Mastery for Strings

A Longitudinal Sequence of Instruction for School Orchestras, Studio Lessons, and College Methods Courses

William Dick and Laurie Scott

Mastery for Strings:
A Longitudinal Sequence of Instruction for School Orchestras,
Studio Lessons, and College Method Courses —
Level One
Copyright © 2018 William Dick and Laurie Scott

ISBN: 978-0-9753919-0-7

Address inquiries to
Mastery for Strings Press
1005 Meriden Lane
Austin, Texas 78703
musipro@aol.com
On the web at www.masteryforstrings.com

Eighth printing 2018
Printed in the United States of America
at OneTouchPoint-Southwest in Austin, Texas

CONTENTS

PREFACE

Teaching a person to play a stringed instrument to a high level of proficiency requires an efficient methodology. Growing young string players to a functional and/or competitive level has been a charge that we have joyfully accepted as a joint project for the past twenty-five years. In addition to our team teaching experiences, our combined sixty years of teaching at preschool through collegiate levels prompted the project of organizing and sequencing exercises and explanations that resulted in the *Mastery for Strings* publication. This approach has consistently and successfully shown students a pathway to independent learning, accurate performance and a comprehensive understanding of string instruments. Although many of our students have taken private instruction from both of us for as many as fifteen years, most have learned in heterogeneous school string class settings with as many as fifty to sixty students.

The complications involved in teaching large heterogeneous string classes also influenced the development of the *Mastery for Strings* approach. The explanation pages and worksheets for each of the steps in the *Mastery for Strings* sequence include clear goals, explicit instructions, and recognizable evaluation criteria. Students must know what is expected of them, how they are to accomplish the expected skills, and what accomplishment, or mastery, looks and sounds like. In a private studio situation this structure can be more easily accomplished. In a large heterogeneous class technical mastery requires more extensive planning. In either setting, a private studio or large string class, the sequence and expected outcomes are the same: there can be no shortcuts for anyone.

A valuable aspect of the *Mastery for Strings* approach is the intentional training of the ability to generalize problem-solving strategies. Students are trained to determine standards of proficiency and self-evaluation skills. These skills help ensure that time spent learning away from the instructor, otherwise known as individual practice, can be efficient and productive. Once students have developed a "standard of excellence" and a method of self-evaluation, the momentum of proceeding from one task to the next without remedial or superfluous drills fosters motivation and provides time for repetition of correct kinesthetic responses.

It is our hope that the *Mastery for Strings* text will provide a methodology for efficient and continuous learning. We define efficient learning as continuous success in presentation of information by the instructor as evidenced by student understanding and performance. *Mastery for Strings* addresses the physical aspects of playing a string instrument and is designed for use in private studios at all levels of instruction, school classrooms and in teacher preparation courses.

THE PEDAGOGICAL PRINCIPLES OF THE MASTERY APPROACH

1. The curriculum is organized into small sequential steps.
2. Students are given a system that encourages effort as the path to success.
3. Music theory (fingerboard geography) is taught to string players without reference to the piano keyboard.
4. Tonality is learned by hearing in-tune examples.
5. Articulation and clarity of tone are nurtured from the beginning of instruction.

6. A sense of pulse and perception of rhythm is based on the internalization of time ratios.
7. Note reading is delayed until reliable posture, tonality and rhythmic perception are established.
8. Advanced technique is learned through review and repetition of previously learned material.

We are grateful to our own teachers, our colleagues, and most especially our students, who have taught us well and provided valuable insight, much pride, and countless hours of great happiness.

—William Dick & Laurie Scott

WHAT IS MASTERY?

The sequence of mastery, as in any sequence of learning, involves stimulus, cognition and response. The acquisition of a skill can be prompted by a stimulus that is aural, visual or imaginative. The imaginative component of the stimulus for learning can be the visualization of task completion or personal creative impulse. The cognitive process is the formation of a physical or kinesthetic plan of action, and the response is the actualization of the cognitive process.

Stimulus
1. **Aural**
2. **Visual**
3. **Imaginative**

Cognition
1. **Knowledge of the entire sequence**
2. **Rationale for learning the task**

Response
1. **Reliable**
2. **Predictable**
3. **Stress-free**
4. **Accurate**

IMPLICATIONS OF THE CONCEPT OF MASTERY IN A LEARNING ENVIRONMENT

In the Mastery Learning environment there exists:
- a teacher or judge
- a student or performer
- a student/performer who acquires the skill to become his/her own teacher/judge
- a sequence of skills to be taught, learned and judged
- a clearly stated Stimulus-Cognition-Response outline or "How To" for each skill
- a standard for task mastery

Mastery demonstrates:
- an understanding of all three stages of the stimulus-cognition-response progression in the accomplishment of a task
- a memory of the cognitive solution that leads to a reliable, predictable, stress-free, accurate response, and the ability to repeat that response
- an honest recognition of success or failure in the stimulus-cognition-response cycle

MASTERY FOR STRINGS

The Mastery Concept includes:
- strategies for specific and efficient teaching
- identifiable goals
- a sequence of what to teach and in what order
- a comprehensive presentation of subject matter
- a way to motivate through expectation
- a standard of quality and definition of excellence
- a belief in student potential
- conceivable outer limits
- opportunities for frequent assessment through the structure of activity
- strategies for training self-evaluation
- knowledge of the interdependence of evaluation and curriculum

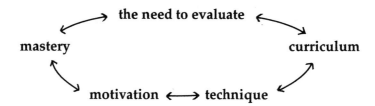

The Mastery Approach capitalizes on:
- self-consciousness or self-awareness
- the want to "keep up" or synchronize
- the impulse to play and compete *
- the need of acceptance from adults and peers
- group synergy
- the fact that environment nurtures growth
- the need for the absence of ambiguity
- children's ability to imitate a model
- the need to know that adults are fair
- the need for feedback that is frequent and brief
- the importance of structure

* A few words on "competition":
There is a theory among anthropologists that earliest civilization may have come about because of the organism's ability to perceive rhythm. That ability led to grunting together, chanting, tribal dancing, social structures, governments, ethics, manners, and society in general. If one accepts the concept of keeping up or trying to synchronize with others, then it becomes a natural opposite that people would notice the differences in each other and would then come to a point of observation: "I have to walk fast to keep up with the group. They move faster than I do." It does seem natural then, that it would become "play" to see who can walk fastest. Observe animals at play. Dogs and horses chase each other to see who can go fastest. Cows walk at the same speed in the same path as part of the same herd. Children and dogs play keep away for fun. From the basic impulse to "keep up" or synchronize comes the ability to observe differences and compete. Competition is a natural thing, and it becomes a negative situation only when the results of competition are assigned values. Group synergy is based and depends on individual differences and strengths.

 Mastery for Strings

The Mastery Approach presents to students:
- optimism about their potential
    "I know you can do this, and I expect accomplishment."
- a scope of learning
    "Here is where we are. Here is where we are going."
- goals that intellectually motivate students with a "presentation of possibility."
- set of finite tasks for learning a string instrument
- a structure that allows every student to progress
- consistent knowledge of progress
- a standard of quality
- the teacher as an ally

The Mastery Approach facilitates:
- frequent feedback
- a concept of excellence and achievement from the first day of instruction
- a standard of quality
- the teaching of technique, not just music
- the development of self-assessment skills
- accelerated skill acquisition without "showing off"
- a commitment to individual development
- persistence and patience
- discipline in skill development
- an appreciation for the abilities and accomplishments of others
- peer tutoring and peer cooperation throughout the development of student evaluation skills
- a method of assessment for students
- a method of assessing whether or not you have taught anything
- review and repetition
- a plan to foster courage instead of anxiety
- a knowledge of process for the purpose of training intuition: applying acquired knowledge to new situations

How To Use This Text

The *Mastery for Strings* text was designed to be used in addition to any of the standard method books available on the market. We found that most method books concentrated on what the student was expected to know, but often did not offer the teacher and student sufficient information on how to accomplish these tasks. *Mastery for Strings* complements these texts by providing detailed explanations of how to achieve technical goals, with stated goals of proficiency.

Each of the pages of *Mastery for Strings* contains instruction for violin, viola, cello, and string bass. Individual step-by-step pedagogical instruction for each instrument is an extremely important aspect of the book, and one that makes it very valuable for heterogeneous string classes and in college teacher preparation courses.

In a school or studio private lesson setting the text can be used as a guide for step-by-step technical mastery for each of the instruments. Each "how-to" page can serve as a lesson note record and practice guide. Mastery charts can be used to set up timelines of accomplishment and mastery.

Each page in the *Mastery for Strings* text represents a step in the sequential development of a string player. Each of these steps can also be broken down into multiple assignments based on the age and experience level of the student involved and the teaching situation. Each page or worksheet is designed to identify a developmental task and a way to solve and evaluate that task according to the following instructional strategy:

1. Choose the technique or skill to be achieved
2. Establish the final expectation
3. Determine the components of that technique or skill
4. Establish the sequence of steps that lead to mastery of that technique or skill
5. Create the checklist or mastery chart to monitor the accomplishment of the technique or skill
6. Develop a schedule or timeline for evaluation with students

The title of each page establishes a label for the technical skill of string playing covered in that lesson. For example, "Tick-Tock Twinkle" is the title on a page that deals with subdivision of a quarter note into eighths and sixteenths, playing with a metronome, and the skill of smooth and staccato bow articulation.

The page continues with "Things You Will Learn": a list of the components necessary to accomplish the goal stated in the "Tick-Tock Twinkle" title.

Things you will learn

- ✔ How to play with a metronome
- ✔ How to play sixteenth notes ♫♫ ♫♫
- ✔ How to play eighth notes ♫ ♫
- ✔ How to play quarter notes ♩ ♩
- ✔ How to make smooth sounds (legato) and stopped sounds (staccato) with your bow
- ✔ How to articulate the bow in "Baroque" style

 Mastery for Strings

The "Rules for Playing" section of each page is a clearly stated list of physical actions that need to be mastered to achieve the skill named in the title of the page.

RULES FOR PLAYING

1. Turn the metronome on to: quarter note equals 60. The metronome will click once each second.
2. Play ♬♬ ♬♬ (rubaduba, rubaduba) on the first note of Twinkle (D). The bow should make a smooth (legato) sound. You will play four bows for each click of the metronome.
3. Play ♫ ♫ (tick-tick-tick-tick) on the second note of Twinkle (A). Each bow stroke should have a strong "T" sound at the beginning of the stroke, and a strong "K" sound at the end of the stroke to make a stopped (staccato) sound. You will play two bows for each click of the metronome.
4. Play ♬♬ ♬♬ (rubaduba, rubaduba) on the third note of Twinkle (B). The bow should make a smooth (legato) sound. You will play four bows for each click of the metronome.
5. Play ♩ ♩ (TOCK - TOCK) on the fourth note of Twinkle (A). Each bow stroke should have a strong "T" sound at the beginning of the stroke, and a strong "K" sound at the end of the stroke to make a stopped (staccato) sound. You will play one bow for each click of the metronome.
6. Continue the rotation of rubaduba, rubaduba; tick-tick-tick-tick; rubaduba, rubaduba; TOCK - TOCK; through all the notes of Twinkle.

Each *Mastery for Strings* page concludes with clear criteria for evaluation so that each student will know how to achieve the goal.

To Achieve Mastery: play Tick-Tock Twinkle with a smooth (legato) bow stroke for all the ♬♬ ♬♬ sixteenth notes, and a stopped (staccato) bow stroke for all the ♫♫♫ eighth and ♩ ♩ quarter notes. The staccato strokes must have a strong "T" sound at the beginning of each stroke and a strong "K" sound at the end of each stroke.

Each page of the *Mastery for Strings* is a lesson plan, a guide for home practice, a document of criteria for accomplishment, and a part of the sequential development of string instrument technique.

The Concept of Mastery and the Grade Book

The traditional system of grading has produced generations of students who calculated what percent of a grade is needed to "pass." This mindset has compromised the concept of mastery and elevated competence to be the norm. Students and parents consider B+ an acceptable grade, but interpreted another way a B+ indicates that a student understands 88% of the course information.

Changing this mindset in education is the goal of the concept of mastery. Rather than accepting a percentage of information acquisition within the time frame of a grading period, the concept of mastery calls for a reorganization of the learning situation that results in understanding and accomplishment of subject matter. This reorganization affects both the presentation of knowledge by the teacher and the self-expectations and responsibilities of the student.

For the teacher the mastery concept requires a detailed curriculum that is sequenced in small, practical, and achievable steps—"mastery items"—coupled with an equally detailed method of evaluation. Both the curriculum and the requirements for mastery must be clearly spelled out and presented to the student, parent, and administration. The student must understand what level of performance is required for mastery, and that partial fulfillment of the goal is not acceptable. Teachers and administrators must believe that each student will succeed through sustained effort.

Grading for mastery compels the teacher to modify the curriculum to fit each classroom and each child. Teachers must be willing to treat each child as an individual learner and each student must be willing to accept the responsibility to accomplish the presented task.

Sample Orchestra Grading Policy

Each grading period contains twelve mastery items arranged in a pedagogical sequence. The mastery items include an equal number of playing skills from the Mastery List and reading skills from any of the standard method books, song books, and orchestra music. Each mastery item has the goal of preparing students for success in school and community or professional orchestras. The student receives a "how-to" page for each mastery item. These pages go into a student orchestra notebook to provide guidance in home practice. Each student also keeps a "mastery chart" in his/her notebook so that status and progress can be checked at any time.

Each student is expected to master each item. If an item is not mastered in the grading period in which it is assigned, then the student keeps working at that skill until it is mastered. If necessary, the teacher and the student should develop an individual mastery sequence, modified to address the skill that needs more time. A commitment of sustained effort from the student must be a component in the development of an individual plan of evaluation. In every case, each student is given the charge of mastery, and each student should complete twelve assignments.

 Mastery for Strings

ORCHESTRA MASTERY CHART

_____ Six Weeks   _____ Period

Student #	Student Name	1	2	3	4	5	6	7	8	9	10	11	12	Total

Masteries:

1. _____   2. _____

3. _____   4. _____

5. _____   6. _____

7. _____   8. _____

9. _____   10 _____

11. _____   12. _____

Level One Mastery List

Put a check mark (✓) in the box for each mastery you achieve.

End of Level One

Mastery for Strings

The Mastery Sequence Divided into Technical Strands
Level One

Strand One: The Left Hand: Form and Flexibility
Goals for Level One:
- a left hand posture that is functional and free of stress
- reliable and accurate intonation
- proper finger action on all four strings with all four fingers
- independent finger action
- "walking" fingers

Level One Masteries: 1; 2; 9-16; 23-28; 30-35; 38-42.

Strand Two: The Bow and Its Repertoire
Goals for Level One:
- a right hand bow hold posture that is functional and free of stress
- flexible finger joints
- free movement from the wrist, elbow, and shoulder
- subdivision of the quarter note beat into eighths, triplets, and sixteenths
- a straight long bow stroke

Level One Masteries: 1; 3-8; 17-22; 29; 36-37.

Strand Three: Cognitive Knowledge of the Fingerboard
Goals for Level One:
- a chromatic scale in two octaves
- twelve one-octave scales
- a knowledge of enharmonic spelling
- a linear and lateral concept of the fingerboard
- an internalization of tonality and intonation
- pitch names by alphabet letters, not finger numbers

Level One Masteries: 12-16; 22-28; 30-35; 38-42; plus solos and orchestra music.

Strand Four: Shifting
Goals for Level One:
- develop a stress-free left hand posture that can move freely up the fingerboard

Level One Masteries: 2; 11; 22.

Strand Five: Vibrato
Goals for Level One:
- develop a stress-free left hand posture

Level One Masteries: 2; 11; 22.

Strand Six: String Crossings
Goals for Level One:
- proper bow arm posture for each string level
- smooth change of string levels

Level One Masteries: 3-8; 17-19; 28; 40.

Strand Seven: Musical Literacy
Goals for Level One:
- internalization of pulse and rhythmic ratios of duration

- a verbal rhythmic counting system
- knowledge of rhythmic notation
- understanding of meter and time signatures
- mental labeling of notes by alphabet name
- thorough knowledge of where notes are on the fingerboard
- knowledge of the function of clef signs
- understanding of how to read lines and spaces
- knowledge of how fingerboard location of pitches are notated on the staff

Level One Masteries: all masteries from strands two and three plus 26 reading assignments from standard method books and orchestral music.

PLACEMENT OF TAPES ON THE FINGERBOARD AND THE BOW

Tapes on the fingerboard:
- help students develop reliable intonation
- help students memorize the kinesthetic distance of half and whole steps
- train the ear to hear the intervals of a half step and a whole step
- assist in developing the ability to project onto the fingerboard a mental grid of note location
- help students develop a knowledge of "fingerboard geography"

Tapes should extend across the whole fingerboard in this pattern (given on the A string):

A String Pitches:	B	Red Tape
	C	Yellow Tape
	C♯	Red Tape
	D	Red Tape
	D♯	Blue Tape
	E	Red Tape

The color of the tapes is entirely arbitrary. Mixing the colors helps to differentiate locations on the fingerboard. When tapes wear off the student should project a mental grid onto the fingerboard.

Tapes on the bow:
- help students identify joints of the arm
- train proper bow distribution

Placement of tapes on the bow:
- yellow tape on the stick to mark the starting point for the ♫♩ rhythm
- red tapes a few inches on either side of the yellow tape to indicate range of motion of this rhythm
- blue tapes to mark the limits of the range of bow motion

REST POSITION AND TAKING A BOW
Mastery #1

Rest position is what you do and how you hold your instrument and bow when you are not playing. There are two kinds of rest position: standing and seated.

STANDING REST POSITION

Violin and Viola

1. Stand with your instrument cradled in your right arm with the back of your violin or viola against your right side. Your elbow will be bent and the side of your right hand will be helping to support the instrument. Be careful that your forearm does not touch the bridge or strings.

2. The scroll of your instrument will be pointing forward and slightly upward.

3. Hang the bow from the first finger of your right hand by placing the tip of your first finger through the frog of the bow. Be sure that the hair of the bow is facing away from you. Place your right thumb on the end of the frog just under the screw of the bow to help you hold the bow tip straight toward the floor.

4. Take a bow by bending your body from the waist. You will be looking right at the floor.

5. Count to three silently and stand up.

To Achieve Mastery: perform the five steps from memory with no mistakes.

Cello and String Bass

1. Stand with the endpin in front of your left foot.

2. Place your left hand carefully around the neck of your instrument and make the body of the cello or bass stand straight up with the strings facing away from you.

3. Hang the bow from the first finger of your right hand by placing the tip of your first finger through the frog of the bow. Be sure that the hair of the bow is facing away from you. Place your right thumb on the end of the frog just under the screw of the bow to help you hold the bow tip straight toward the floor.

4. Step to the side of your instrument so that you can comfortably take a bow by bending your body from the waist. You will be looking right at the floor.

5. Count to three silently and stand up.

To Achieve Mastery: perform the five steps from memory with no mistakes.

SEATED REST POSITION

Violin and Viola

1. Sit on the edge of your chair with your feet flat on the floor and your back straight.

2. Place the instrument on your left knee with the strings facing away from you.

3. Place your left hand lightly on the left shoulder of the instrument with your fingers across the strings and your thumb across the back of the violin or viola.

4. Hold your bow lightly in the palm of your right hand (do not touch the hair of the bow). Place your hand on your right knee with the tip of the bow pointing straight up in the air.

To Achieve Mastery: perform the four steps from memory with no mistakes.

Cello

1. Adjust the endpin so that when you stand the scroll of the cello is at head level.

2. Stand with the endpin in front of your left foot, cello facing away from you.

3. Sit on the edge of your chair so that your feet are in front of the chair legs. Your knees will be separated.

4. Hold the cello with your left hand, at arm's length in front of you.

5. Bring the cello to your body so that the neck is to the left of your head, the "C" tuning peg is just behind your left ear, and the right shoulder of the cello is resting against the center of your chest. The fingerboard should be straight up and down and your knees should be holding the back edges of the cello just below where the bow is going to travel.

6. Place your left hand lightly on the shoulder of the cello on the A string side of the fingerboard.

7. Hold your bow lightly in the palm of your right hand (do not touch the hair of the bow). Place your hand on your right knee with the tip of the bow pointing straight up in the air.

To Achieve Mastery: perform the seven steps from memory with no mistakes.

String Bass

1. Adjust the endpin so that when you stand the bottom of the scroll is at head level.

2. Stand so that the leg of the stool is between your heels.

3. Sit on the edge of your stool. Place your left foot on the rung of the stool, and place your right foot flat on the floor.

4. Place the bass so that the back edges of the instrument touch both your legs.

5. Turn the bass (clockwise) and bring the instrument in towards your body until the back edge of the bass touches your stomach and the back of the bass is resting against your left thigh.

6. Hold the bow in your right hand and let it hang by your right side.

To Achieve Mastery: perform the six steps from memory with no mistakes.

   Mastery for Strings

How to Hold the Instrument
Mastery #2

VIOLIN AND VIOLA

1. Begin at standing rest position.
2. Place your left thumb across the back of the instrument and let your fingers curve across the front of the instrument.
3. With the instrument in your left hand, hold it out to the left side of your body.
4. Adjust your feet to be slightly apart until you have good balance.
5. Swing the instrument (counter-clockwise) until the tail button is at "ten minutes after the hour."
6. Bring the tail button to the front of your left ear, then slowly guide the instrument down until it rests on top of your left shoulder. Keep looking straight ahead.
7. Turn your head to the left until your chin comes to rest on the chin rest. Nod your head "yes" and place all the weight of your head on the chin rest.
8. Drop your left hand and place it on your right shoulder. You will be holding the instrument in the "Look Ma! No hands!" position.
9. With the help of your left hand make a good bow hold with your right hand.
10. Place your left hand on the neck of your instrument in playing position.
11. Place your bow on the A string. Use the tape nearest the frog to place the bow halfway between the bridge and the fingerboard.

To Achieve Mastery: perform the eleven steps from memory with no mistakes.

CELLO

1. Begin at seated rest position.
2. Place your arms around the shoulders of the cello in a gentle "hug."
3. Drop your arms to your side and gently rock the cello back and forth from side to side with your knees while saying "Look Ma! No hands!"
4. Using your left hand as a helper, make a good bow hold.
5. Place your left hand on the neck of the cello in good playing position.
6. Place your bow on the A string. Use the tape nearest the frog to place the bow halfway between the bridge and the fingerboard.

To Achieve Mastery: perform the six steps from memory with no mistakes.

STRING BASS

1. Begin at seated rest position.
2. Balance the bass against your body and your leg. Drop your arms to your side and gently rock the bass back and forth from side to side with your legs and say "Look Ma! No hands!"
3. Using your left hand as a helper, make a good bow hold.
4. Put your left hand on the neck of the bass in good playing position.
5. Place your bow on the G string. Use the tape nearest the frog to place the bow halfway between the bridge and the fingerboard.

To Achieve Mastery: perform the five steps from memory with no mistakes.

How To Use Your Left Hand
Mastery #2, continued

VIOLIN AND VIOLA

1. Make a "stop" sign with your left hand.
2. Turn your "stop" sign around until it faces you.
3. Notice that your thumb pad is facing you.
4. Swing your elbow from your shoulder toward the middle of your body until your forearm bone is pointing straight up.
5. Locate the crease or line at the base of your first finger. This line is placed on the right side of the neck of the instrument behind the first tape. Place your hand so that the crease touches the neck exactly where the black wood is glued to the white wood.
6. Place your thumb on the left side of the neck. The pad of your thumb will face you (stop sign) and the side of your thumb pad will touch the neck.
7. Curl your first finger until it lands exactly on the first tape. Your fingernail should be facing you just like a mirror. You should see the string coming out under the left corner of your fingernail.
8. Pick up your first finger so that the fingernail floats above the tape like a balloon. Adjust your hand so that all your fingernails float above the string.

To Achieve Mastery: perform the eight steps from memory with no mistakes.

CELLO AND STRING BASS

1. Make a "stop" sign.
2. Turn the "stop" sign until it faces you.
3. Locate your thumb pad.
4. Pick up your elbow until the stop sign faces the floor.
5. Pivot your elbow joint until the stop sign floats above the fingerboard.
6. Slide the fingers over the fingerboard and place the fingertips of all four fingers on the tapes. Your fingernails should be facing the side of your face.
7. Let the side of your thumb pad touch the left side of the neck under your second finger.

To Achieve Mastery: perform the seven steps from memory with no mistakes.

 Mastery for Strings

How To Hold the Bow
Mastery #3

1. Take hold of the stick of the bow with your left hand, being careful not to touch the hair of the bow. Hold the stick in the middle of the bow with the frog toward the right side of your body.

2. Extend your right arm straight out from your shoulder with your thumb pointing toward the ceiling.

3. "Bend" the thumb on your right hand.

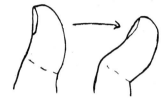

4. "Bend" the fingers of your right hand from the middle joint.

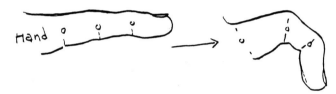

5. Rotate your forearm bone counter-clockwise until the palm of your hand is parallel with the floor. Be careful not to raise your elbow.

6. Place the frog of the bow into your right hand so that the pad of your ring finger covers the "eye" of the frog; the tip of your middle finger is just touching the "lip" of the frog; the crease of your first knuckle is touching the wrapping of the bow; and your little finger is sitting on top of the stick.*

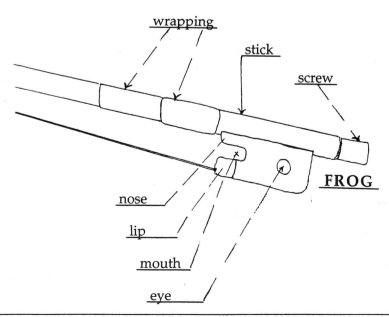

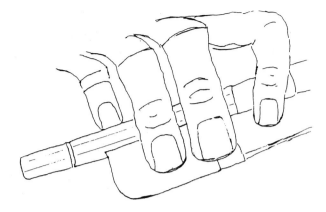

7. Push "bent" thumb into the frog's "nose." The inside corner of your thumb will touch the bottom of the bow stick, and the end of your thumb will touch the "nose" of the frog. Your thumbnail will be looking out between the stick and the hair. Be very careful that your thumbnail does not look at the floor. Your bow hand will sit flat on the stick, just like a bird on a wire.

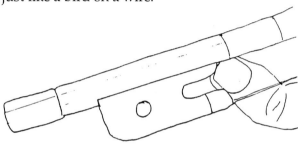

8. Turn your arm so that the tip of the bow is pointed toward the ceiling. Drop your left arm to your side and present your Bow Hold.

To Achieve Mastery: perform the eight steps from memory with no mistakes.

* Cellists and string bass players using a French Bow will eventually change the little finger posture so that the pad of the finger touches the top of the stick. This change should be delayed until right hand finger strength is developed.

GERMAN BOW HOLD FOR STRING BASS PLAYERS

1. Take hold of the stick of the bow with your left hand, being careful not to touch the hair of the bow. Hold the stick in the middle of the bow with the frog toward the right side of your body.
2. Reach around the bow and place the stick of the bow between the tips of the first two fingers of your right hand, very much like holding an arrow.
3. Bend your ring finger into the "mouth" of the frog.
4. Place the side of your little finger on the "lip" of the frog.
5. Place the pad of your thumb on the top of the stick.
6. Turn your arm so that the tip of the bow is pointed toward the ceiling. Drop your left arm to your side and present your Bow Hold.

To Achieve Mastery: perform the six steps from memory with no mistakes.

Copyright ©2004 William Dick & Laurie Scott   *Mastery for Strings*

BOW GAMES: WINDSHIELD WIPERS
Mastery #4

THINGS YOU WILL LEARN

✔ To pivot the bow from your elbow, without raising your shoulder.

✔ To take the weight of the bow on your little finger.

RULES FOR PLAYING

1. This game is played without your instrument.
2. Make your best bow hold holding the tip toward the ceiling.
3. Stretch your instrument hand out in front of you with the palm up.
4. Pivot the bow from your elbow until the tip of the bow rests in the palm of your instrument hand.
5. Make sure that your bow hold stays in the same shape.
6. You will notice the weight of the bow on the end of your little finger.
7. Repeat 25 times.

To Achieve Mastery: perform the seven steps from memory with no mistakes.

BOW GAMES: JETÉ–PLIÉ
Mastery #5

THINGS YOU WILL LEARN

✔ Terms used in ballet ("jeté" and "plié") to describe how to use your fingers on the bow.

✔ Exact placement for your fingers and thumb for a perfect bow hold.

✔ How to keep your bow hand soft and flexible.

RULES FOR PLAYING

1. Hold your bow stick at arm's length with your instrument hand at the middle of the stick.
2. Make your best bow hold.
3. On the command "Jeté" take your thumb, first finger, and little finger off the frog and straighten the "knees" of your two middle fingers. Stick your thumb, little finger and first finger straight out into the air. There will be tension in your fingers and thumb.
4. On the command "Plié" bend the "knees" of your two middle fingers so that the backs of your fingers, hand, wrist, and forearm are all in a flat plane.
5. On the command "Set" return your thumb, little finger, and first finger to exactly the right spot for your best bow hold. Release all tension in your fingers and thumb. The bow hold is the relaxed state. You now have completed the plié motion.
6. Repeat 25 times.

To Achieve Mastery: perform the six steps from memory with no mistakes.

Bow Games: Santa Rita
Mastery #6

Things You Will Learn

✔ That Santa Rita was the first oil well in Texas.

✔ How to simulate the see-saw motion of an oil well with your bow.

✔ The "plié" bow hold is the proper hold for the frog; the "jeté" bow hold is the proper hold for the tip.

✔ Your fingers must be soft and flexible for the bow to be able to pivot on the end of the thumb.

Rules For Playing

1. Place the bow at the frog on the bridge in "plié" position; let half of the hair be on either side of the bridge.

2. Violas on the C string. Cellos on the A string. Violins on the G string. Basses on G.

3. Using the end of your thumb as the pivot point, "jeté" little finger and let the frog of the bow **rock** to the other side of the strings (violins to E, violas to A, cellos to C, basses to E). Your other fingers will "jeté" also, but not as much as your pinkie.

4. Reverse the motion ("plié" your little finger) and let the bow **roll** back to its original starting place.

5. Do not pull the bow; you should not make any sound.

6. Repeat 25 times.

To Achieve Mastery: perform the six steps from memory with no mistakes.

 Mastery for Strings

Bow Games: Edward ScissorBow
Mastery #7

Things You Will Learn

✔ That the place where the hair of the bow touches the string of your instrument is called "the point of contact."

✔ How to let the bow slide up and down the fingerboard.

✔ How to pull the bow back behind the bridge.

✔ How to control "the point of contact" of your bow hair and the string of your instrument.

✔ Violin and Viola: When your bow is at the frog, your bow hold is like the moment when the bow tip slides down the fingerboard; when your bow is at the tip, your bow hold is like the moment when your bow tip is behind the bridge.

✔ Cello and Bass: When your bow is at the frog, your bow hold is like the moment when the bow is behind the bridge; when your bow is at the tip, your bow hold is like the moment when your bow is pulled up over the fingerboard.

✔ Your fingers must be soft and flexible for the bow to be able to pivot on the end of the thumb.

Rules For Playing

1. Place the bow on any string halfway between the middle of the bow and the tip.

2. Violin and Viola: Using the end of your thumb as the pivot point, let the tip of the bow slide down over the fingerboard. Your little finger will be very curved ("plié") and your first finger and thumb will be almost straight ("jeté").

   Cello and Bass: Using the end of your thumb as the pivot point, pull the tip of the bow up over the fingerboard. Your little finger will be straight ("jeté") and your first finger will be curved ("plié").

3. Violin and Viola: Reverse the motion and pull the tip of the bow back until the bow slides behind the bridge. Your little finger will be straight ("jeté") and your first finger and thumb will be curved ("plié").

   Cello and Bass: Reverse the motion and let the bow slide down behind the bridge. Your little finger will be very curved ("plié") and your first finger will be straight ("jeté").

4. Return the bow to usual playing position.

5. Repeat 25 times.

To Achieve Mastery: perform the five steps from memory with no mistakes.

BOW GAMES: BOW TAPS
Mastery #8

THINGS YOU WILL LEARN

✔ How to let the bow move inside your bow hold.

✔ How to let the end of your thumb function as a "fulcrum" or "pivot point" for lifting the bow off the string.

✔ How the tip and the frog of the bow move in opposition.

✔ The ♪♪♪ ♫ rhythm is called the "Taka Taka Stop Stop" or "Taka" rhythm.

RULES FOR PLAYING

1. Make a good bow hold.

2. Place your bow hair on the string exactly in the middle of the bow. Violins set on the A string. Violas, cellos, and basses set on the D string.

3. Let the bow stick roll on the end of your thumb as you "jeté" your little finger. When you do this the tip of the bow will come up in the air. Notice that the frog goes toward the floor and the tip goes toward the ceiling. Your thumb is acting as the "fulcrum" or "pivot point."

4. Release the "jeté" of your little finger and the bow will fall back onto the string. Notice the feeling of the bow rolling on the end of your thumb.

5. Repeat this motion and your bow will "tap" the string. You will be producing almost no sound, only the sound of the hair tapping the string.

6. Play the ♪♪♪ ♫ rhythm on each of your open strings. Say the name of the string before you play.

How is this game different from Windshield Wipers? In this game the "fulcrum" moves to the end of your thumb. In Windshield Wipers the fulcrum was your elbow joint.

To Achieve Mastery: perform the six steps from memory with no mistakes.

FLOWER AND MONKEY SONGS

THINGS YOU WILL LEARN

- ✔ How to use your fingers on the fingerboard of your instrument.
- ✔ How to change the bow from one string to another.
- ✔ The names of the notes your fingers play.

RULE FOR PLAYING

Play the ♪♪♪♪ ♪♪ rhythm on each note on the specified string.

Flower Song
Mastery #9

VIOLIN

E string:	E	F♯	E	
A string:				A

VIOLA AND CELLO

A string	A	B	A	
D string:				D

STRING BASS

G string:	A	B	A	
D string:				D

Monkey Song
Mastery #10

VIOLIN, VIOLA, AND CELLO

A string:	A	B	C♯	D	D	C♯	B	A

STRING BASS

G string:				G	G			
D string:	D	E	F♯			F♯	E	D

(used with the permission of Marilyn O'Boyle)

To Achieve Mastery: perform Flower Song and Monkey Song from memory with no mistakes.

HOW TO USE THE FINGERS OF YOUR INSTRUMENT HAND
Mastery #11

GENERAL RULE: Play on the tips of your fingers

DEFINITION: FINGERCUT — THE DENT IN THE END OF YOUR FINGER MADE WHEN YOU PRESS DOWN THE STRING

1. The thumb touches the neck of the instrument on the inside corner of the thumbnail. Violin/viola: thumb touches the side of the neck opposite the 1st finger. Cello/bass: thumb touches the back of the neck opposite the 2nd finger.
2. No other part of the thumb can touch the neck of the instrument.
3. The wrist must be straight.
4. The knuckles must <u>stand up</u>. When the fingers are pressed down they form little "chairs."
5. The fingercut must be in the correct place.

Violin and Viola

Cello and String Bass

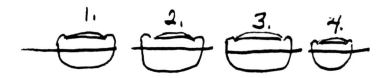

TIP: Tapes are helpers for playing in tune.

To Achieve Mastery: perform Flower Song and Monkey Song from memory with perfect "fingercuts."

Copyright ©2004 William Dick & Laurie Scott   *Mastery for Strings*

OPEN ESCALATOR SONG
Masteries #12–15

THINGS YOU WILL LEARN

✔ How to play notes that are a half step apart with the same finger (second finger).
✔ How to hear a half step interval and a whole step interval.
✔ How to develop a flexible first joint in your fingers.
✔ That the string bass is too large to have escalator fingering.

RULES FOR PLAYING THE ESCALATOR SONG

1. Say the name of each note before you play it.
2. Once you have used a finger, keep it down on the fingerboard.
3. When you reach the top of the escalator pattern, repeat that note and go down the escalator (the note names will be in reverse order).
4. Open string escalators stay on the same string.
5. The finger that plays the half step escalator (or "shifts") slides on the string: do not pick your finger up and jump.
6. Play the ♩♫♫ ♩♩ rhythm on each note.

Open Escalator Patterns:

Mastery #12—

Open string escalator on A:	A	B	C	C♯	D
Finger numbers (violin/viola)	0	1	2	2	3
Finger numbers (string bass)	0	1	2	4	1 (basses shift to III Pos. for D)

* cellist see below

Mastery #13—

Open string escalator on D:	D	E	F	F♯	G (basses shift to III Pos. for G)

Mastery #14—

Open string escalator on G:	G	A	B♭	B	C (basses shift to III Pos. for C)

Mastery #15—

Open string escalator on C:	C	D	E♭	E	F

Open string escalator on E:	E	F♯	G	G♯	A (basses shift to III Pos. for A)

*Special instructions for cellist: Cello players ride the escalator in two ways:

Open string escalator on A :	A	B	C	C♯	D
Finger numbers:	0	1	2	3	4

Open string escalator on A with extension fingering:

	A	B	C	C♯	D
Finger numbers:	0	1	2	X2	3

*Ride the escalator with both your second finger and your thumb.

To Achieve Mastery: ride the escalator on all four strings, saying the name of the note before you play it and have only one fingercut on each finger.

OPEN ESCALATOR TEST
Test of Masteries #12–15

NAME _____ **INSTRUMENT** _____

Write the names of the notes of the escalator on the blanks and then place the notes on the music staff. Be sure to start with the name of the open string, and also be sure to draw your clef sign before you draw the notes.

Notes on the A string:

____ ____ ____ ____ ____

Notes on the D string:

____ ____ ____ ____ ____

Notes on the G string:

____ ____ ____ ____ ____

Notes on the C string:

____ ____ ____ ____ ____

Notes on the E string:

____ ____ ____ ____ ____

Study Guides for the Open Escalator Test appear on the following pages.
Teachers have permission to copy this page for classroom use.

   Mastery for Strings

STUDY GUIDE FOR OPEN ESCALATOR TEST
INSTRUMENT—VIOLIN

Write the names of the notes of the escalator on the blanks and then place the notes on the music staff. Be sure to start with the name of the open string, and also be sure to draw your clef sign before you draw the notes.

Notes on the A string:

Notes on the D string:

Notes on the G string:

Notes on the E string:

To Achieve Mastery: play and write all the escalators perfectly.

STUDY GUIDE FOR OPEN ESCALATOR TEST
INSTRUMENT—VIOLA

Write the names of the notes of the escalator on the blanks and then place the notes on the music staff. Be sure to start with the name of the open string, and also be sure to draw your clef sign before you draw the notes.

Notes on the A string:

Notes on the D string:

Notes on the G string:

Notes on the C string:

To Achieve Mastery: play and write all the escalators perfectly.

Copyright ©2004 William Dick & Laurie Scott   *Mastery for Strings*

STUDY GUIDE FOR OPEN ESCALATOR TEST
INSTRUMENT—CELLO

Write the names of the notes of the escalator on the blanks and then place the notes on the music staff. Be sure to start with the name of the open string, and also be sure to draw your clef sign before you draw the notes.

Notes on the A string:

Notes on the D string:

Notes on the G string:

Notes on the C string:

To Achieve Mastery: play and write all the escalators perfectly.

STUDY GUIDE FOR OPEN ESCALATOR TEST
INSTRUMENT—STRING BASS

Write the names of the notes of the escalator on the blanks and then place the notes on the music staff. Be sure to start with the name of the open string, and also be sure to draw your clef sign before you draw the notes.

Notes on the A string:

Notes on the D string:

Notes on the G string:

Notes on the E string:

To Achieve Mastery: play and write all the escalators perfectly.

Copyright ©2004 William Dick & Laurie Scott   *Mastery for Strings*

ONE-OCTAVE SCALES THAT START ON AN OPEN STRING:
SCALE SET I
Mastery #16

DEFINITIONS

• A scale is a series of consecutive pitches.

• An octave is the pitch eight notes higher or lower from the starting pitch. Since we only use seven letters of the alphabet, the name of the octave pitch is always the same as the beginning pitch.

THINGS YOU WILL LEARN

✔ What a scale is.

✔ What the word "octave" means.

✔ How to play a "Major Scale."

RULES FOR PLAYING

1. Say the name of the pitch before you play it.
2. Play the ♩♩♩ ♩♩ rhythm on each note of the scale.
3. When you reach the top pitch, repeat that pitch and then play back down the scale.

One-octave open string scales:

A	B	C♯	D	E	F♯	G♯	A
D	E	F♯	G	A	B	C♯	D
G	A	B	C	D	E	F♯	G
C	D	E	F	G	A	B	C

Play the scales listed below for your instrument:

Violins: A, D, G
Violas: D, G, C
Cellos: D, G, C
String Basses: C   start 2nd finger on the A string
G   start 2nd finger on the E string

To Achieve Mastery: you may look at this page to perform the scales for your instrument with no mistakes.

MASTERY AND READING MUSIC NOTATION

When students can demonstrate the ability to play with good posture, consistently correct intonation, and a sense of internal pulse and rhythmic ratios, music reading should be introduced.

The written language of music is broken into two components:
- Pitch symbols which notate the logic system of music tonality
- Rhythmic symbols which notate the mathematical ratios of duration

What is expected in a music reading situation?
- a knowledge of fingerboard geography
- a perception of pulse and rhythmic ratios
- an understanding of symbols that represent pitch and duration
- pitch notation perceived as a fingerboard location for the left hand and a string level for the right hand
- pitch symbols processed as alphabet names, not finger numbers
- rhythmic notation related to bow speed for the right arm
- rhythmic notation processed into a verbal counting system
- the stimulus-cognition-response sequence occuring simultaneously within a regulated tempo

Stimulus:
Notation

                Cognition:
                  Location on the fingerboard
                  Duration (bow speed)
                  String level (bow)

                              Response:
                              Sound/music

 Mastery for Strings

Twinkle Twinkle Little Star
(Alphabet Twinkle)

For Violin, Viola, and Cello

A String:			A	A	B	B	A						
D String:	D	D						G	G	F#	F#	E	E	D

A String:	A	A			
D String:			G	G	F#	F#	E

A String:	A	A			
D String:			G	G	F#	F#	E

A String:		A	A	B	B	A
D String:	D	D						G	G	F#	F#	E	E	D

For String Bass

G String:			A	A	B	B	A	G	G
D String:	D	D								F#	F#	E	E	D

G String:	A	A	G	G
D String:				F#	F#	E

G String:	A	A	G	G
D String:				F#	F#	E

G String:		A	A	B	B	A	G	G
D String:	D								F#	F#	E	E	D

Mastery for Strings   Copyright ©2004 William Dick & Laurie Scott   31

STUDY GUIDE FOR TWINKLE TEST

TWINKLE TWINKLE LITTLE STAR

FILL IN THE BLANKS WITH THE NOTE THAT PLAYS THE WORD OR SYLLABLE

D	D	A	A	B	B	A
Twin	kle	twin	kle	lit	tle	star

G	G	F♯	F♯	E	E	D
How	I	won	der	what	you	are

A	A	G	G	F♯	F♯	E
Up	a	bove	the	world	so	high

A	A	G	G	F♯	F♯	E
Like	a	dia	mond	in	the	sky

D	D	A	A	B	B	A
Twin	kle	twin	kle	lit	tle	star

G	G	F♯	F♯	E	E	D
How	I	won	der	what	you	are

Twinkle Twinkle Little Star is a folk song that has four phrases. Phrases in music are like sentences in language and usually have a complete thought.

In *Twinkle Twinkle Little Star*—
Phrase one is the words: Twinkle twinkle little star, how I wonder what you are.
Phrase two is: Up above the world so high.
Phrase three is: Like a diamond in the sky.
Phrase four repeats the words: Twinkle twinkle little star, how I wonder what you are.

You can notice that the notes in phrases one and four are exactly the same, and that the notes in phrases two and three are exactly the same.

 Mastery for Strings

TWINKLE TEST

NAME _____

TWINKLE TWINKLE LITTLE STAR

FILL IN THE BLANKS WITH THE NOTE THAT PLAYS THE WORD OR SYLLABLE

| Twin | kle | twin | kle | lit | tle | star |

| How | I | won | der | what | you | are |

| Up | a | bove | the | world | so | high |

| Like | a | dia | mond | in | the | sky |

| Twin | kle | twin | kle | lit | tle | star |

| How | I | won | der | what | you | are |

Teachers have permission to copy this page for classroom use.

STUDY GUIDE FOR TWINKLE COOKBOOK TEST

On the "Twinkle Test" page you learned that the song *Twinkle Twinkle Little Star* has four phrases. You also learned that phrases one and four are exactly alike; they even have the same words. In "Twinkle Cookbook" we call these phrases "bread." You also learned that phrases two and three have exactly the same notes even though the words are different. In "Twinkle Cookbook" we call these phrases "cheese."

WRITE THE RECIPE FOR "BREAD"

D	D	A	A	B	B	A
G	G	F♯	F♯	E	E	D

WRITE THE RECIPE FOR "CHEESE"

A	A	G	G	F♯	F♯	E

MAKE A TWINKLE SANDWICH BY PLAYING THE RECIPE FOR "BREAD"

D	D	A	A	B	B	A
G	G	F♯	F♯	E	E	D

NEXT ADD TWO SLICES OF "CHEESE"

A	A	G	G	F♯	F♯	E
A	A	G	G	F♯	F♯	E

FINISH THE TWINKLE SANDWICH BY PLAYING ONE MORE "BREAD"

D	D	A	A	B	B	A
G	G	F♯	F♯	E	E	D

Congratulations: You have just played Twinkle Twinkle Little Star.

Copyright ©2004 William Dick & Laurie Scott *Mastery for Strings*

TWINKLE COOKBOOK TEST

NAME _____

WRITE THE RECIPE FOR "BREAD"

___ ___ ___ ___ ___ ___ ___

___ ___ ___ ___ ___ ___ ___

WRITE THE RECIPE FOR "CHEESE"

___ ___ ___ ___ ___ ___ ___

MAKE A TWINKLE SANDWICH BY PLAYING THE RECIPE FOR "BREAD"

___ ___ ___ ___ ___ ___ ___

___ ___ ___ ___ ___ ___ ___

NEXT ADD TWO SLICES OF "CHEESE"

___ ___ ___ ___ ___ ___ ___

___ ___ ___ ___ ___ ___ ___

FINISH THE TWINKLE SANDWICH BY PLAYING ONE MORE "BREAD"

___ ___ ___ ___ ___ ___ ___

___ ___ ___ ___ ___ ___ ___

Teachers have permission to copy this page for classroom use.

TWINKLE COOKBOOK WITH FINGER NUMBERS

VIOLIN AND VIOLA

Recipe for "Bread"

A string:			0	0	1	1	0
D string:	0		0				
D string:	3		3	2	2	1	1	0

Recipe for "Cheese"

A string:	0	0					
D string:			3	3	2	2	1

CELLO

Recipe for "Bread"

A string:			0	0	1	1	0
D string:	0		0				
D string:	4	4	3	3	1	1	0

Recipe for "Cheese"

A string:	0	0					
D string:			4	4	3	3	1

STRING BASS

Recipe for "Bread"

G string:			1	1	4	4	1
D string:	0	0					
G string:	0	0					
D string:			4	4	1	1	0

Recipe for "Cheese"

G string:	1	1	0	0			
D string:					4	4	1

Compose a complete Twinkle Sandwich by playing: Bread-Cheese-Cheese-Bread

 Mastery for Strings

STUDY GUIDE FOR CLEF SIGN TEST

VIOLIN

My clef sign is called the __TREBLE__ clef.

It identifies the __SECOND__ line as the pitch __G__.

That is why the __TREBLE__ clef is nicknamed the __G__ clef.

VIOLA

My clef sign is called the __ALTO__ clef.

It identifies the __THIRD__ line as the pitch __C__.

That is why the __ALTO__ clef is nicknamed the __C__ clef.

CELLO AND STRING BASS

My clef sign is called the __BASS__ clef.

It identifies the __FOURTH__ line as the pitch __F__.

That is why the __BASS__ clef is nicknamed the __F__ clef.

STUDY GUIDE FOR
HOW TO READ THE LINES AND SPACES OF THE STAFF

TREBLE CLEF (G CLEF)

Once my clef sign has identified the __SECOND__ line as the pitch __G__,

I can read the other lines and spaces of the staff by going __FORWARD__

through the alphabet if I read __UP__ the staff or by going __BACKWARD__

through the alphabet if I read __DOWN__ the staff.

ALTO CLEF (C CLEF)

Once my clef sign has identified the __THIRD__ line as the pitch __C__,

I can read the other lines and spaces of the staff by going __FORWARD__

through the alphabet if I read __UP__ the staff or by going __BACKWARD__

through the alphabet if I read __DOWN__ the staff.

BASS CLEF (F CLEF)

Once my clef sign has identified the __FOURTH__ line as the pitch __F__,

I can read the other lines and spaces of the staff by going __FORWARD__

through the alphabet if I read __UP__ the staff or by going __BACKWARD__

through the alphabet if I read __DOWN__ the staff.

NAME _____ INSTRUMENT _____

CLEF SIGN TEST

Fill in the blanks for your instrument.

My clef sign is called the _____ clef.

It identifies the _____ line as the pitch _____.

That is why the _____ clef is nicknamed the _____ clef.

TEST
HOW TO READ THE LINES AND SPACES OF THE STAFF

Fill in the blanks.

Once my clef sign has identified the _____ line as the pitch _____,

I can read the other lines and spaces of the staff by going _____

through the alphabet if I read _____ the staff or by going _____

through the alphabet if I read _____ the staff.

Teachers have permission to copy this page for classroom use.

 Mastery for Strings

TAKA TWINKLE
Masteries #17–19

THINGS YOU WILL LEARN

- ✔ How to play an entire folk song.
- ✔ **Mastery #17**— How to have a good bow hold at the frog of the bow (plié).
- ✔ **Mastery #18**— How to have a good bow hold at the middle of the bow.
- ✔ **Mastery #19**— How to have a good bow hold at the tip of the bow (jeté).
- ✔ How to use different joints of your bow arm for different parts of the bow.

RULES FOR PLAYING

1. Play the ♫♫ ♩♩ on each note of Twinkle Twinkle Little Star in the middle of the bow using your bow tapes as guides. Your bow hold should be balanced and all fingers and thumb should be curved. Your bow arm will move from the elbow joint.

2. Play the ♫♫ ♩♩ on each note of Twinkle Twinkle Little Star at the frog of the bow. Your bow hold should be in the "plié" position. Your bow arm will swing from the shoulder joint.

3. Play the ♫♫ ♩♩ on each note of Twinkle, Twinkle Little Star at the tip of the bow. Your bow hold should be in the "jeté" position. Your bow arm will use a combination of all the joints.

To Achieve Mastery: play the entire folk song Twinkle Twinkle Little Star at the frog, middle, and tip of the bow.

Pitch names for Taka Twinkle (play the ♫♫ ♩♩ rhythm on each of these notes):

D	A	B	A	G	F♯	E	D
A	G	F♯	E				
A	G	F♯	E				
D	A	B	A	G	F♯	E	D

BOW GAMES: SILENT BOW LANDING
Mastery #20

THINGS YOU WILL LEARN

✔ That the bow hand is in the "plié" posture at the frog, and the "jeté" posture at the tip.

✔ How to support the weight of the bow when the bow is off the instrument and still keep a good bow hold.

✔ How to circle the bow.

✔ The symbols for down bow (⊓) and up bow (V).

RULES FOR PLAYING

1. You must know the notes to Twinkle.

2. Make a good bow hold and place your bow on the instrument at the frog. Make sure your bow hand is in the "plié" posture.

3. Play each note of Twinkle on a down bow stroke (⊓).

4. Circle the bow after each note and reset it at the frog without making any sound. That is why this game is called Silent Bow Landing. Remember to check your "plié" posture each time you set the bow.

5. Repeat the notes of Twinkle on an up bow stroke(V) by placing your bow on the instrument at the tip of the bow. Make sure your bow hand is in the "jeté" posture. Circle the bow after each note and reset it at the tip without making any sound. Remember to check your "jeté" posture each time you set the bow.

To Achieve Mastery: perform the five steps from memory with no mistakes.

     Mastery for Strings

BOW GAMES: ARCO-PIZZICATO TWINKLE
Mastery #21

THINGS YOU WILL LEARN

- ✔ "Arco" means to produce tone with the hair of the bow.
- ✔ "Pizzicato" means to produce tone by picking the string with the fingers of the right bow hand.
- ✔ How to change from arco to pizzicato quickly.
- ✔ How to make a clear pizzicato sound.

RULES FOR PLAYING

1. You must know the notes for Twinkle.
2. You must know the proper bow position for playing pizzicato.
3. Play Twinkle alternating arco and pizzicato on each new pitch.

BOW GAMES: ARCO-LEFT-HAND PIZZICATO TWINKLE

THINGS YOU WILL LEARN

- ✔ How to make a clear left-hand pizzicato sound.
- ✔ How to make your left-hand posture strong enough to hold down a finger and play pizzicato with another finger in the same hand.

RULES FOR PLAYING

1. Play Twinkle as before but play the pizzicato notes with the fingers of your left hand.
2. Cellos must play G pizzicato with their bow hand.
3. Basses must play B and F# pizzicato with their bow hand.

To Achieve Mastery: perform both versions of arco-pizzicato Twinkle from memory alternating bowed and pizzicato notes with no mistakes.

LONG-BOW TWINKLE
Mastery #22

To Achieve Mastery: use your bow to play Twinkle so that it sounds exactly the same as if you were singing it.

ELEVATOR SONG: SET I
Masteries #23–27

THINGS YOU WILL LEARN

✔ The name of the note each finger plays on each of the strings.

✔ How to use walking fingers when crossing from one string to another string.

✔ How to use your instrument arm to play in the same fingercut on all strings.

RULES FOR PLAYING ELEVATOR SONG

1. Say the names of the two notes on each string before you play them.

2. Place the new finger before you lift the old finger.

3. Keep your instrument arm free so that it will rotate to deliver your fingercut to the new string.

4. Start on lowest string and play the pattern on each string. Get off the elevator after the highest string and check to see that you have only one fingercut. Get back on the elevator, repeat the top string and go down (note names will be in reverse order).

5. Play the first note as ♫♫ and the second note as ♩.

Elevator Patterns: All patterns are given on the A string.

Mastery #23—
Set I, no. 1:   A - B   open and 1

Mastery #24—
Set I, no. 2:   B - C   1 and half step 2

Mastery #25—
Set I, no. 3:   B - C♯   1 and whole step 2 for violins and violas; 1 and 3 or extended 2 for cellos; 1 and 4 for basses

Mastery #26—
Set I, no. 4:   C - D   2 and whole step 3 for violins and violas; 2 and 4 for cellos; 1 and 4 in II position for basses

Mastery #27—
Set I, no. 5:   C♯ - D   2 and half step 3 for violins and violas; 3 and 4 or extended 2 and 3 for cellos; 2 and 4 in II position for basses

To Achieve Mastery: ride all five of the elevators in 3 and 1/2 minutes and have one fingercut on each finger.

To play the Elevator Song as an orchestra, the cellos and violas start on the C string; violins and string basses join on the G string; everyone plays the D and A string; cellos and violas wait for the E string and then rejoin the Elevator Song on the A string; cellos and violas finish on the C string.

Note that the string basses ride the Elevator from the top to the bottom when playing with the class.

     Mastery for Strings

SET I ELEVATOR TEST
Test of Masteries #23–27

NAME _____ **INSTRUMENT**_____

WRITE THE NOTES FOR THE _____ _____ **ELEVATOR.**

Remember that the pattern for the elevator is given on the A String.

Fingering for this elevator pattern is _____ and _____ in _____ Position.

Going Up

IV String   _____   _____

III String   _____   _____

II String   _____   _____

I String   _____   _____

Coming Down

I String   _____   _____

II String   _____   _____

III String   _____   _____

IV String   _____   _____

WRITE THE NOTES FOR THIS ELEVATOR ON THE STAFF.

Remember that what goes *Up* must come *Down*.

Up: _____

Down: _____

Study Guides for the Set I Elevator Test appear on the following pages.

Teachers have permission to copy this page for classroom use.

STUDY GUIDE for Elevator Test—VIOLIN—Set I, no. 1—Mastery #23

WRITE THE NOTES FOR THE ___A___ ___B___ ELEVATOR.

Remember that the pattern for the elevator is given on the A String.
Fingering for this elevator pattern is ___0___ and ___1___ in ___I___ Position.

Going Up			**Coming Down**		
IV String	G	A	I String	F♯	E
III String	D	E	II String	B	A
II String	A	B	III String	E	D
I String	E	F♯	IV String	A	G

WRITE THE NOTES FOR THIS ELEVATOR ON THE STAFF.

Remember that what goes *Up* must come *Down*.

Up:

Down:

STUDY GUIDE for Elevator Test—VIOLIN—Set I, no. 2—Mastery #24

WRITE THE NOTES FOR THE ___B___ ___C___ ELEVATOR.

Remember that the pattern for the elevator is given on the A String.
Fingering for this elevator pattern is ___1___ and ___2___ in ___I___ Position.

Going Up			**Coming Down**		
IV String	A	B♭	I String	G	F♯
III String	E	F	II String	C	B
II String	B	C	III String	F	E
I String	F♯	G	IV String	B♭	A

WRITE THE NOTES FOR THIS ELEVATOR ON THE STAFF.

Remember that what goes *Up* must come *Down*.

Up:

Down:

Copyright ©2004 William Dick & Laurie Scott   *Mastery for Strings*

STUDY GUIDE for Elevator Test—VIOLIN—Set I, no. 3—Mastery #25

WRITE THE NOTES FOR THE ___B___ ___C#___ **ELEVATOR.**

Remember that the pattern for the elevator is given on the A String.
Fingering for this elevator pattern is ___1___ and ___2___ in ___I___ Position.

Going Up			**Coming Down**		
IV String	A	B	I String	G#	F#
III String	E	F#	II String	C#	B
II String	B	C#	III String	F#	E
I String	F#	G#	IV String	B	A

WRITE THE NOTES FOR THIS ELEVATOR ON THE STAFF.

Remember that what goes *Up* must come *Down*.

Up:

Down:

STUDY GUIDE for Elevator Test—VIOLIN—Set I, no. 4—Mastery #26

WRITE THE NOTES FOR THE ___C___ ___D___ **ELEVATOR.**

Remember that the pattern for the elevator is given on the A String.
Fingering for this elevator pattern is ___2___ and ___3___ in ___I___ Position.

Going Up			**Coming Down**		
IV String	B♭	C	I String	A	G
III String	F	G	II String	D	C
II String	C	D	III String	G	F
I String	G	A	IV String	C	B♭

WRITE THE NOTES FOR THIS ELEVATOR ON THE STAFF.

Remember that what goes *Up* must come *Down*.

Up:

Down:

WRITE THE NOTES FOR THE ___C♯___ ___D___ ELEVATOR.

Remember that the pattern for the elevator is given on the A String.
Fingering for this elevator pattern is ___2___ and ___3___ in ___I___ Position.

Going Up		
IV String	B	C
III String	F♯	G
II String	C♯	D
I String	G♯	A

Coming Down		
I String	A	G♯
II String	D	C♯
III String	G	F♯
IV String	C	B

WRITE THE NOTES FOR THIS ELEVATOR ON THE STAFF.

Remember that what goes *Up* must come *Down*.

Up:

Down:

     Mastery for Strings

STUDY GUIDE for Elevator Test—VIOLA—Set I, no. 1—Mastery #23

WRITE THE NOTES FOR THE ___A___ ___B___ **ELEVATOR.**

Remember that the pattern for the elevator is given on the A String.
Fingering for this elevator pattern is ___0___ and ___1___ in ___I___ Position.

Going Up

IV String	C	D
III String	G	A
II String	D	E
I String	A	B

Coming Down

I String	B	A
II String	E	D
III String	A	G
IV String	D	C

WRITE THE NOTES FOR THIS ELEVATOR ON THE STAFF.

Remember that what goes *Up* must come *Down*.

Up:

Down:

STUDY GUIDE for Elevator Test—VIOLA—Set I, no. 2—Mastery #24

WRITE THE NOTES FOR THE ___B___ ___C___ **ELEVATOR.**

Remember that the pattern for the elevator is given on the A String.
Fingering for this elevator pattern is ___1___ and ___2___ in ___I___ Position.

Going Up

IV String	D	E♭
III String	A	B♭
II String	E	F
I String	B	C

Coming Down

I String	C	B
II String	F	E
III String	B♭	A
IV String	E♭	D

WRITE THE NOTES FOR THIS ELEVATOR ON THE STAFF.

Remember that what goes *Up* must come *Down*.

Up:

Down:

STUDY GUIDE for Elevator Test—VIOLA —Set I, no. 3—Mastery #25

WRITE THE NOTES FOR THE   __B__   __C♯__   **ELEVATOR.**

Remember that the pattern for the elevator is given on the A String.
Fingering for this elevator pattern is __1__ and __2__ in __I__ Position.

Going Up			**Coming Down**		
IV String	D	E	I String	C♯	B
III String	A	B	II String	F♯	E
II String	E	F♯	III String	B	A
I String	B	C♯	IV String	E	D

WRITE THE NOTES FOR THIS ELEVATOR ON THE STAFF.

Remember that what goes *Up* must come *Down*.

Up:

Down:

STUDY GUIDE for Elevator Test—VIOLA —Set I, no. 4—Mastery #26

WRITE THE NOTES FOR THE   __C__   __D__   **ELEVATOR.**

Remember that the pattern for the elevator is given on the A String.
Fingering for this elevator pattern is __2__ and __3__ in __I__ Position.

Going Up			**Coming Down**		
IV String	E♭	F	I String	D	C
III String	B♭	C	II String	G	F
II String	F	G	III String	C	B♭
I String	C	D	IV String	F	E♭

WRITE THE NOTES FOR THIS ELEVATOR ON THE STAFF.

Remember that what goes *Up* must come *Down*.

Up:

Down:

    Mastery for Strings

STUDY GUIDE for Elevator Test—VIOLA —Set I, no. 5—Mastery #27

WRITE THE NOTES FOR THE _____C♯_____ _____D_____ **ELEVATOR.**

Remember that the pattern for the elevator is given on the A String.
Fingering for this elevator pattern is ___2___ and ___3___ in ___I___ Position.

Going Up

IV String	E	F
III String	B	C
II String	F♯	G
I String	C♯	D

Coming Down

I String	D	C♯
II String	G	F♯
III String	C	B
IV String	F	E

WRITE THE NOTES FOR THIS ELEVATOR ON THE STAFF.

Remember that what goes *Up* must come *Down*.

Up:

Down:

STUDY GUIDE for Elevator Test—CELLO—Set I, no. 1—Mastery #23

WRITE THE NOTES FOR THE _____A_____ _____B_____ **ELEVATOR.**

Remember that the pattern for the elevator is given on the A String.
Fingering for this elevator pattern is _____0_____ and _____1_____ in _____I_____ Position.

Going Up			**Coming Down**		
IV String	C	D	I String	B	A
III String	G	A	II String	E	D
II String	D	E	III String	A	G
I String	A	B	IV String	D	C

WRITE THE NOTES FOR THIS ELEVATOR ON THE STAFF.

Remember that what goes *Up* must come *Down*.

Up:

Down:

STUDY GUIDE for Elevator Test—CELLO —Set I, no. 2—Mastery #24

WRITE THE NOTES FOR THE _____B_____ _____C_____ **ELEVATOR.**

Remember that the pattern for the elevator is given on the A String.
Fingering for this elevator pattern is _____1_____ and _____2_____ in _____I_____ Position.

Going Up			**Coming Down**		
IV String	D	E♭	I String	C	B
III String	A	B♭	II String	F	E
II String	E	F	III String	B♭	A
I String	B	C	IV String	E♭	D

WRITE THE NOTES FOR THIS ELEVATOR ON THE STAFF.

Remember that what goes *Up* must come *Down*.

Up:

Down:

Mastery for Strings

STUDY GUIDE for Elevator Test—CELLO —Set I, no. 3—Mastery #25

WRITE THE NOTES FOR THE _____B_____ _____C♯_____ **ELEVATOR.**

Remember that the pattern for the elevator is given on the A String.
Fingering for this elevator pattern is _____1_____ and _____3_____ in _____I_____ Position.

Going Up			**Coming Down**		
IV String	D	E	I String	C♯	B
III String	A	B	II String	F♯	E
II String	E	F♯	III String	B	A
I String	B	C♯	IV String	E	D

WRITE THE NOTES FOR THIS ELEVATOR ON THE STAFF.

Remember that what goes *Up* must come *Down*.

Up:

Down:

STUDY GUIDE for Elevator Test—CELLO —Set I, no. 4—Mastery #26

WRITE THE NOTES FOR THE _____C_____ _____D_____ **ELEVATOR.**

Remember that the pattern for the elevator is given on the A String.
Fingering for this elevator pattern is _____2_____ and _____4_____ in _____I_____ Position.

Going Up			**Coming Down**		
IV String	E♭	F	I String	D	C
III String	B♭	C	II String	G	F
II String	F	G	III String	C	B♭
I String	C	D	IV String	F	E♭

WRITE THE NOTES FOR THIS ELEVATOR ON THE STAFF.

Remember that what goes *Up* must come *Down*.

Up:

Down:

STUDY GUIDE for Elevator Test—CELLO —Set I, no. 5—Mastery #27

WRITE THE NOTES FOR THE __C♯__ __D__ **ELEVATOR.**

Remember that the pattern for the elevator is given on the A String.
Fingering for this elevator pattern is __3__ and __4__ in __I__ Position.

Going Up

IV String	E	F
III String	B	C
II String	F♯	G
I String	C♯	D

Coming Down

I String	D	C♯
II String	G	F♯
III String	C	B
IV String	F	E

WRITE THE NOTES FOR THIS ELEVATOR ON THE STAFF.

Remember that what goes *Up* must come *Down*.

Up:

Down:

Mastery for Strings

STUDY GUIDE for Elevator Test—STRING BASS—Set I, no. 1—Mastery #23

WRITE THE NOTES FOR THE _____A_____ _____B_____ **ELEVATOR.**

Remember that the pattern for the elevator is given on the A String.
Fingering for this elevator pattern is _____0_____ and _____1_____ in _____I_____ Position.

Going Up

IV String	E	F♯
III String	A	B
II String	D	E
I String	G	A

Coming Down

I String	A	G
II String	E	D
III String	B	A
IV String	F♯	E

WRITE THE NOTES FOR THIS ELEVATOR ON THE STAFF.

Remember that what goes *Up* must come *Down*.

Up:

Down:

STUDY GUIDE for Elevator Test—STRING BASS —Set I, no. 2—Mastery #24

WRITE THE NOTES FOR THE _____B_____ _____C_____ **ELEVATOR.**

Remember that the pattern for the elevator is given on the A String.
Fingering for this elevator pattern is _____1_____ and _____2_____ in _____I_____ Position.

Going Up

IV String	F♯	G
III String	B	C
II String	E	F
I String	A	B♭

Coming Down

I String	B♭	A
II String	F	E
III String	C	B
IV String	G	F♯

WRITE THE NOTES FOR THIS ELEVATOR ON THE STAFF.

Remember that what goes *Up* must come *Down*.

Up:

Down:

STUDY GUIDE for Elevator Test—STRING BASS —Set I, no. 3—Mastery #25

WRITE THE NOTES FOR THE _____B_____ _____C♯_____ **ELEVATOR.**

Remember that the pattern for the elevator is given on the A String.
Fingering for this elevator pattern is ___1___ and ___4___ in ___I___ Position.

Going Up

IV String	F♯	G♯
III String	B	C♯
II String	E	F♯
I String	A	B

Coming Down

I String	B	A
II String	F♯	E
III String	C♯	B
IV String	G♯	F♯

WRITE THE NOTES FOR THIS ELEVATOR ON THE STAFF.

Remember that what goes *Up* must come *Down*.

Up:

Down:

STUDY GUIDE for Elevator Test—STRING BASS —Set I, no. 4—Mastery #26

WRITE THE NOTES FOR THE _____C_____ _____D_____ **ELEVATOR.**

Remember that the pattern for the elevator is given on the A String.
Fingering for this elevator pattern is ___1___ and ___4___ in ___II___ Position.

Going Up

IV String	G	A
III String	C	D
II String	F	G
I String	B♭	C

Coming Down

I String	C	B♭
II String	G	F
III String	D	C
IV String	A	G

WRITE THE NOTES FOR THIS ELEVATOR ON THE STAFF.

Remember that what goes *Up* must come *Down*.

Up:

Down:

Mastery for Strings

WRITE THE NOTES FOR THE <u> C♯ </u> <u> D </u> **ELEVATOR.**

Remember that the pattern for the elevator is given on the A String.
Fingering for this elevator pattern is <u> 2 </u> and <u> 4 </u> in <u> II </u> Position.

Going Up			**Coming Down**		
IV String	G♯	A	I String	C	B
III String	C♯	D	II String	G	F♯
II String	F♯	G	III String	D	C♯
I String	B	C	IV String	A	G♯

WRITE THE NOTES FOR THIS ELEVATOR ON THE STAFF.

Remember that what goes *Up* must come *Down*.

Up:

Down:

EXPRESS ELEVATORS: SET I
Mastery #28

THINGS YOU WILL LEARN

✔ The names of the notes in each elevator pattern.

✔ How to play the elevator pattern in tune across the fingerboard.

✔ How to play across the fingerboard and have one fingercut.

✔ How to slur across the entire fingerboard with smooth arm motion.

RULES FOR PLAYING

Separate bows:
1. Say the name of all the notes in the elevator, up and down, before you play.
2. After playing the elevator check to see that you have only one fingercut on each finger.
3. Remember to use walking fingers as you cross the fingerboard.

Slurred bows:
1. Say the name of all the notes in the elevator, up and down, before you play.
2. After playing the elevator check to see that you have only one fingercut on each finger.
3. Remember to use walking fingers as you cross the fingerboard.
4. The frog of your bow should make a smooth arc as you slur across the strings.
5. The bow should not "click" from one string level to the next string level.

To Achieve Mastery: ride each of the elevator patterns on all four strings, saying the names of the notes before you play them and have only one fingercut on each finger.

Set I Elevators: Remember that the pattern is given on the A string.
1. A - B
2. B - C
3. B - C♯
4. C - D
5. C♯ - D

         Mastery for Strings

EXPRESS ELEVATOR SET I—VIOLIN—MASTERY #28

Remember that the notenames for the patterns are given on the A string.

Separate bows

Slurred Express Elevators

Remember that the notenames for the patterns are given on the A string.

Separate bows

A-B (open to first finger)

B-C (first to second finger)

B-C# (first to second finger)

C-D (second to third finger)

C#-D (second to third finger)

Slurred Express Elevators

A-B (open to first finger)

B-C (first to second finger)

B-C# (first to second finger)

C-D (second to third finger)

C#-D (second to third finger)

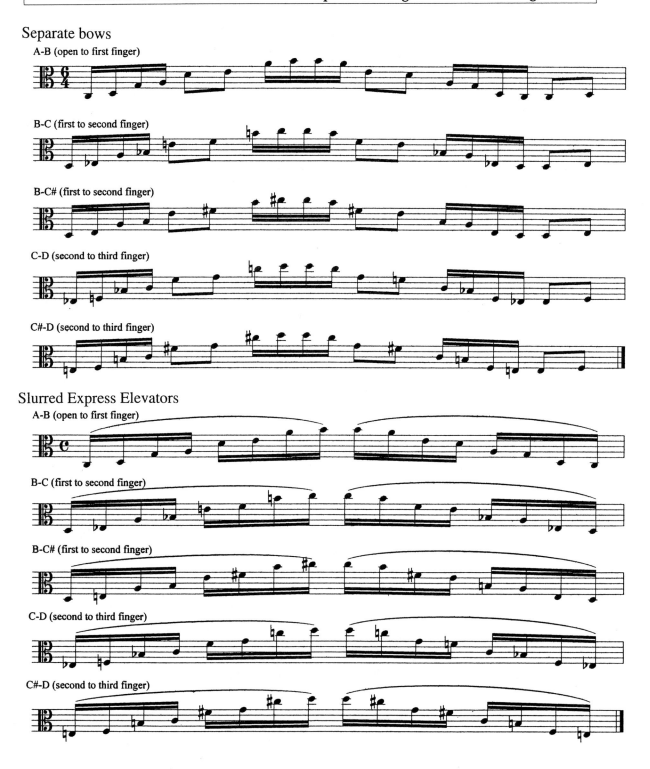

Copyright ©2004 William Dick & Laurie Scott   *Mastery for Strings*

EXPRESS ELEVATOR SET I—CELLO—MASTERY #28

Remember that the notenames for the patterns are given on the A string.

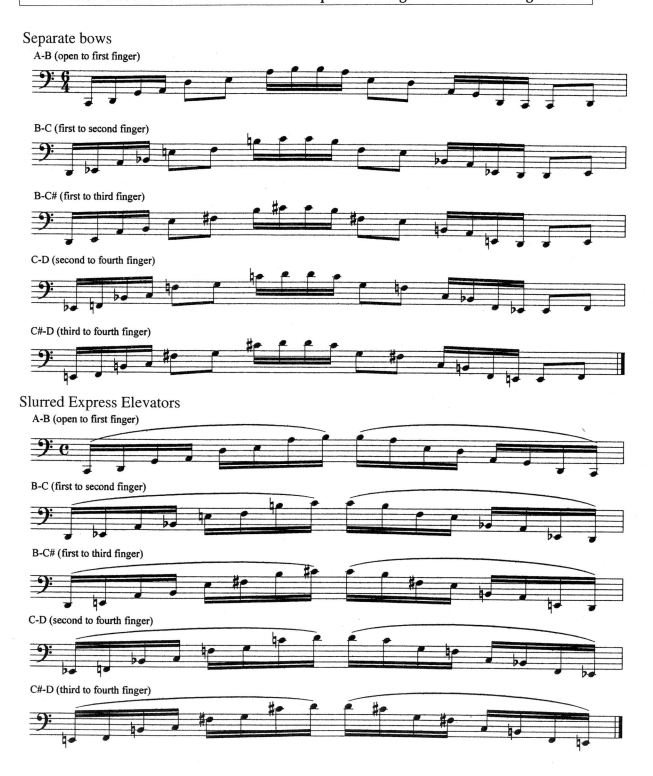

EXPRESS ELEVATOR SET I
STRING BASS, SOLO VERSION—MASTERY #28

Remember that the notenames for the patterns are given on the A string.

Separate bows

A-B (open to first finger)

B-C (first to second finger)

B-C# (first to fourth finger)

C-D (first to fourth finger in II position)

C#-D (second to fourth finger in II position)

Slurred Express Elevators

A-B (open to first finger)

B-C (first to second finger)

B-C# (first to fourth finger)

C-D (first to fourh finger in II position)

C#-D (second to fourth finger in II position)

  Mastery for Strings

EXPRESS ELEVATOR SET I
STRING BASS, CLASS VERSION—MASTERY #28

Remember that the notenames for the patterns are given on the A string.

Separate bows

A-B (open to first finger)

B-C (first to second finger)

B-C# (first to fourth finger)

C-D (first to fourth finger in II position)

C#-D (second to fourth finger in II position)

Slurred Express Elevators

A-B (open to first finger)

B-C (first to second finger)

B-C# (first to fourth finger)

C-D (first to fourh finger in II position)

C#-D (second to fourth finger in II position)

RHYTHM ROUND TWINKLE
Mastery #29

THINGS YOU WILL LEARN

✔ What a rhythmic sequence is.

✔ How to play Twinkle in half (𝅗𝅥), quarter (𝅘𝅥), and eighth (𝅘𝅥𝅮) notes.

✔ The mathematical ratios between half, quarter, and eighth notes.

RULES FOR PLAYING

1. Play the first word of "Twinkle" as two half notes: 𝅗𝅥   𝅗𝅥

2. Play the second "Twinkle" as four quarter notes: 𝅘𝅥 𝅘𝅥   𝅘𝅥 𝅘𝅥

3. Play the word "Little" as eight eighth notes: 𝅘𝅥𝅮𝅘𝅥𝅮 𝅘𝅥𝅮𝅘𝅥𝅮   𝅘𝅥𝅮𝅘𝅥𝅮 𝅘𝅥𝅮𝅘𝅥𝅮

4. Play the word "Star" as two half notes: 𝅗𝅥   𝅗𝅥

5. Continue through the rest of the song with the half note, quarter note, eighth note sequence

6. Combine with other players to perform Rhythm Round Twinkle as an orchestra.

To Achieve Mastery: perform the first five steps from memory with no mistakes.

NOTES FOR RHYTHM ROUND TWINKLE ON THE FOLLOWING PAGES

RHYTHM ROUND TWINKLE FOR ORCHESTRA
Mastery #29, continued

Copyright ©2004 William Dick & Laurie Scott *Mastery for Strings*

FIRST FINGER ESCALATOR SONG
Masteries #30 & 31

THINGS YOU WILL LEARN

✔ How to play notes that are a half step apart with the same finger (third finger for violin and viola). Cellos learn how to use a forward second extension (X-2) to achieve the escalator pattern.
✔ How to "transpose" the escalator pattern to a different starting note.
✔ How to hear a half step interval and a whole step interval.
✔ How to develop a flexible first joint in your fingers.
✔ How to use the fourth finger on violin and viola.
✔ That the string bass is too large to have escalator fingering.

RULES FOR PLAYING THE ESCALATOR SONG

1. Say the name of each note before you play it.
2. Once you have used a finger, keep it down on the fingerboard.
3. When you reach the top of the escalator pattern, repeat that note and go down the escalator (the note names will be in reverse order).
4. First finger escalators stay on the same string.
5. The finger that plays the half step escalator (or shifts) slides on the string: do not pick your finger up and jump.
6. Play the ♪♪♪ ♩♩ rhythm on each note.

Escalator Patterns:

Mastery #30—

First finger escalator on A:	B	C♯	D	D♯	E	
Finger numbers (violin/viola)	1	2	3	3	4	
Finger numbers (cello)	1	X2	3	4	1	(shift to IV Pos. for E)
Finger numbers (string bass)	1	4	1	2	4	(shift to III. Pos. for D)
			0	1	2	(half position on D string)

First finger escalator on D:	E	F♯	G	G♯	A	(basses and cellist shift)
			0	1	2	(basses also use half position)

Mastery #31—

First finger escalator on G:	A	B	C	C♯	D	(basses and cellist shift)

First finger escalator on C:	D	E	F	F♯	G	(cellist shift)

First finger escalator on E:	F♯	G♯	A	A♯	B	(basses shift to III Pos. for A)
			0	1	2	(basses also use half position)

Special instructions for cellist: Remember that your second finger and your thumb ride together when you use extension fingering.

To Achieve Mastery: ride the escalator on all four strings, saying the name of the note before you play it and have only one fingercut on each finger.

Copyright ©2004 William Dick & Laurie Scott *Mastery for Strings*

FIRST FINGER ESCALATOR TEST
Test of Masteries #30 & 31

NAME _____ **INSTRUMENT**_____

Write the names of the notes of the escalator on the blanks and then place the notes on the music staff. Be sure to draw your clef sign before you draw the notes.

Notes on the A string:

____   ____   ____   ____   ____

Notes on the D string:

____   ____   ____   ____   ____

Notes on the G string:

____   ____   ____   ____   ____

Notes on the C string:

____   ____   ____   ____   ____

Notes on the E string:

____   ____   ____   ____   ____

**Study Guides for the First Finger Escalator Test appear on the following pages.
Teachers have permission to copy this page for classroom use.**

STUDY GUIDE FOR FIRST FINGER ESCALATOR TEST
INSTRUMENT—VIOLIN

Write the names of the notes of the escalator on the blanks and then place the notes on the music staff. Be sure to start with the name of the open string, and also be sure to draw your clef sign before you draw the notes.

Notes on the A string:

Notes on the D string:

Notes on the G string:

Notes on the E string:

To Achieve Mastery: play and write all the escalators perfectly.

Mastery for Strings

STUDY GUIDE FOR FIRST FINGER ESCALATOR TEST
INSTRUMENT—VIOLA

Write the names of the notes of the escalator on the blanks and then place the notes on the music staff. Be sure to draw your clef sign before you draw the notes.

Notes on the A string:

Notes on the D string:

Notes on the G string:

Notes on the C string:

To Achieve Mastery: play and write all the escalators perfectly.

STUDY GUIDE FOR FIRST FINGER ESCALATOR TEST
INSTRUMENT—CELLO

Write the names of the notes of the escalator on the blanks and then place the notes on the music staff. Be sure to draw your clef sign before you draw the notes.

Notes on the A string:

Notes on the D string:

Notes on the G string:

Notes on the C string:

To Achieve Mastery: play and write all the escalators perfectly.

Mastery for Strings

STUDY GUIDE FOR FIRST FINGER ESCALATOR TEST
INSTRUMENT—STRING BASS

Write the names of the notes of the escalator on the blanks and then place the notes on the music staff. Be sure to draw your clef sign before you draw the notes.

Notes on the A string:

Notes on the D string:

Notes on the G string:

Notes on the E string:

To Achieve Mastery: play and write all the escalators perfectly.

ONE-OCTAVE SCALES THAT START ON FIRST FINGER: SCALE SET II
Mastery #32

DEFINITIONS

- A scale is a series of consecutive pitches.
- An octave is the pitch eight notes higher or lower from the starting pitch. Since we only use seven letters of the alphabet, the name of the octave pitch is always the same as the beginning pitch.

THINGS YOU WILL LEARN

✔ What a scale is.

✔ What the word octave means.

✔ How to play a "Major Scale."

RULES FOR PLAYING

1. Say the name of the note before you play it.
2. Play the ♫♫ ♩♩ rhythm on each note of the scale.
3. When you reach the top pitch, repeat that pitch and then play back down the scale.

One-octave first finger scales:

B	C♯	D♯	E	F♯	G♯	A♯	B
E	F♯	G♯	A	B	C♯	D♯	E
A	B	C♯	D	E	F♯	G♯	A
D	E	F♯	G	A	B	C♯	D

Play the scales listed below for your instrument:

Violins: B, E, A

Violas: E, A, D

Cellos: E, A, D   cello first-finger scales use 2nd finger in extension, and the final note is played with 1st finger in 4th position

Basses: D, A, E   bass scales start on open strings and shift to III position

To Achieve Mastery: you may look at this page to perform the scales for your instrument with no mistakes.

    Mastery for Strings

RING TONE ESCALATOR SONG
Masteries #33 & 34

THINGS YOU WILL LEARN

✔ How the octave notes of the open strings produce "Ring Tones."
✔ How to play notes that are a half step apart with the same finger (first finger). Cellos learn how to use a backward first finger extension (X-1) to achieve the escalator pattern.
✔ How to "transpose" the escalator pattern to a different starting note.
✔ How to hear a half step interval and a whole step interval.
✔ How to develop a flexible first joint in your fingers.

RULES FOR PLAYING THE ESCALATOR SONG

1. Say the name of each note before you play it.
2. Once you have used a finger, keep it down on the fingerboard.
3. When you reach the top of the escalator pattern, repeat that note and go down the escalator (the note names will be in reverse order).
4. Ring Tone escalators use two strings. The Ring Tone Escalator always starts on the string that is one lower than where the pattern ends. Example: the A string Ring Tone Escalator starts on the D string (E string for basses).
5. The finger that plays the half step escalator (or shifts) slides on the string: do not pick your finger up and jump.
6. Play the ♫♫ ♩♩ rhythm on each note.

Escalator Patterns

Remember that the Ring Tone Escalator always starts on the next lower string.

Mastery #33—

Ring Tone Escalator on A	G	A	B♭	B	C	
Finger numbers (violin/viola)	3	0	1	1	2	
Finger numbers (cello)	4	0	X1	1	2	
Finger numbers (string bass)	2	0	1	1	2	(at last, an escalator)
Finger numbers (string bass)	2	0	1	2	4	(remain in half-position)
Ring Tone Escalator on D	C	D	E♭	E	F	

Mastery #34—

Ring Tone Escalator on G	F	G	A♭	A	B♭
Violins have to imagine a C string					
Ring Tone Escalator on C	(_)	C	D♭	D	E♭
Violas and cellos have to imagine an F string					
Ring Tone Escalator on E	D	E	F	F♯	G

Special instructions for cellist: To do a first finger escalator simply point your first finger back toward you ear and place the finger on the string, and then slide it to its usual posture to ride the escalator. Your thumb does not go back with your first finger extension. Review open escalator for first finger posture.

To Achieve Mastery: ride the escalator on all four strings, saying the name of the note before you play it and have only one fingercut on each finger.

STUDY GUIDE FOR RING TONE ESCALATOR TEST
INSTRUMENT—VIOLIN

Write the names of the notes of the escalator on the blanks and then place the notes on the music staff. Be sure to draw your clef sign before you draw the notes.

Notes on the A string & D string:

Notes on the D string & G string:

Notes on the G string:

Notes on the E string & A string:

To Achieve Mastery: play and write all the escalators perfectly.

     Mastery for Strings

RING TONE ESCALATOR TEST
INSTRUMENT—VIOLIN
TEST OF MASTERIES #33 & 34

NAME _____

Write the names of the notes of the escalator on the blanks and then place the notes on the music staff. Be sure to draw your clef sign before you draw the notes.

Notes on the A string & D string:

____   ____   ____   ____   ____

Notes on the D string & G string:

____   ____   ____   ____   ____

Notes on the G string:

____   ____   ____   ____   ____

Notes on the E string & A string:

____   ____   ____   ____   ____

Teachers have permission to copy this page for classroom use.

STUDY GUIDE FOR RING TONE ESCALATOR TEST
INSTRUMENT—VIOLA

Write the names of the notes of the escalator on the blanks and then place the notes on the music staff. Be sure to draw your clef sign before you draw the notes.

Notes on the A string & D string:

G   A   B♭   B   C

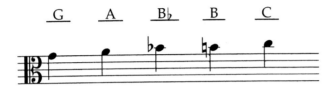

Notes on the D string & G string:

C   D   E♭   E   F

Notes on the G string & C string:

F   G   A♭   A   B♭

Notes on the C string:

𝄽   C   D♭   D   E♭

To Achieve Mastery: play and write all the escalators perfectly.

Mastery for Strings

NAME _____

Write the names of the notes of the escalator on the blanks and then place the notes on the music staff. Be sure to draw your clef sign before you draw the notes.

Notes on the A string & D string:

____   ____   ____   ____   ____

Notes on the D string & G string:

____   ____   ____   ____   ____

Notes on the G string & C string:

____   ____   ____   ____   ____

Notes on the C string:

____   ____   ____   ____   ____

Teachers have permission to copy this page for classroom use.

STUDY GUIDE FOR RING TONE ESCALATOR TEST
INSTRUMENT—CELLO

Write the names of the notes of the escalator on the blanks and then place the notes on the music staff. Be sure to draw your clef sign before you draw the notes.

Notes on the A string & D string:

G   A   B♭   B   C

Notes on the D string & G string:

C   D   E♭   E   F

Notes on the G string & C string:

F   G   A♭   A   B♭

Notes on the C string:

𝄽   C   D♭   D   E♭

To Achieve Mastery: play and write all the escalators perfectly.

    Mastery for Strings

RING TONE ESCALATOR TEST
INSTRUMENT—CELLO
TEST OF MASTERIES #33 & 34

NAME _____

Write the names of the notes of the escalator on the blanks and then place the notes on the music staff. Be sure to draw your clef sign before you draw the notes.

Notes on the A string & D string:

____ ____ ____ ____ ____

Notes on the D string & G string:

____ ____ ____ ____ ____

Notes on the G string & C string:

____ ____ ____ ____ ____

Notes on the C string:

____ ____ ____ ____ ____

Teachers have permission to copy this page for classroom use.

Write the names of the notes of the escalator on the blanks and then place the notes on the music staff. Be sure to draw your clef sign before you draw the notes.

Notes on the A string & E string:

<u>G</u>   <u>A</u>   <u>B♭</u>   <u>B</u>   <u>C</u>

Notes on the D string & A string:

<u>C</u>   <u>D</u>   <u>E♭</u>   <u>E</u>   <u>F</u>

Notes on the G string & D string:

<u>F</u>   <u>G</u>   <u>A♭</u>   <u>A</u>   <u>B♭</u>

Notes on the E string:

<u>𝄽</u>   <u>E</u>   <u>F</u>   <u>F♯</u>   <u>G</u>

To Achieve Mastery: play and write all the escalators perfectly.

Mastery for Strings

RING TONE ESCALATOR TEST
INSTRUMENT—STRING BASS
TEST OF MASTERIES #33 & 34

NAME _____

Write the names of the notes of the escalator on the blanks and then place the notes on
the music staff. Be sure to draw your clef sign before you draw the notes.

Notes on the A string & E string:

____ ____ ____ ____ ____

Notes on the D string & A string:

____ ____ ____ ____ ____

Notes on the G string & D string:

____ ____ ____ ____ ____

Notes on the E string:

____ ____ ____ ____ ____

Teachers have permission to copy this page for classroom use.

ELEVATOR SONG: SET II
Mastery #35

THINGS YOU WILL LEARN

✔ The name of the note each finger plays on each of the strings.

✔ How to use walking fingers when crossing from one string to another string.

✔ How to use your instrument arm to play in the same fingercut on all strings.

RULES FOR PLAYING

1. Say the names of the two notes on each string before you play them.

2. Place the new finger before you lift the old finger.

3. Keep your instrument arm free so that it will rotate to deliver your fingercut to the new string.

4. Start on lowest string and play the pattern on each string. Get off the elevator after the highest string and check to see that you have only one fingercut. Get back on the elevator, repeat the top string and go down (note names will be in reverse order).

5. Play the first note as 4 sixteenths, and the second note as 2 eighths.

Elevator Patterns: All patterns are given on the A string.

Set II, no. 1: A - B♭   open and 1 in 1/2 position

Set II, no. 2: B♭ - C   1 in 1/2 position and whole step 2 for violins and violas; X-1 and 2 for cello; 1 and 4 for basses

Set II, no. 3: C♯ - D♯   2 and whole step 3 for violins and violas; extended 2 and 4 for cellos; 1 and 4 for basses in II Position

Set II, no. 4: D - E   3 and whole step 4 for violins and viola; 2 and 4 in II Position for cellos; 1 and 4 in III Position for basses

Set II, no. 5: D♯ - E   3 and half step 4 for violins and violas; 3 and 4 in II Position for cellos; 2 and 4 in III Position for basses

Set II, no. 6: D - E♭   3 and half step 4 for violins and violas; 2 and 3 in II Position for cellos; 1 and 2 in III Position for basses

To Achieve Mastery: ride all six of the elevators in 4 minutes and have one fingercut on each finger.

 Mastery for Strings

SET II ELEVATOR TEST
Test of Mastery #35

NAME _____ INSTRUMENT_____

WRITE THE NOTES FOR THE _____ _____ ELEVATOR.

Remember that the pattern for the elevator is given on the A String.

Fingering for this elevator pattern is _____ and _____ in _____ Position.

Going Up

IV String   _____   _____

III String   _____   _____

II String   _____   _____

I String   _____   _____

Coming Down

I String   _____   _____

II String   _____   _____

III String   _____   _____

IV String   _____   _____

WRITE THE NOTES FOR THIS ELEVATOR ON THE STAFF.

Remember that what goes *Up* must come *Down*.

Up:

Down:

Study Guides for the Set II Elevator Test appear on the following pages.

Teachers have permission to copy this page for classroom use.

STUDY GUIDE for Set II Elevator Test—VIOLIN—Set II, no. 1

WRITE THE NOTES FOR THE   A   B♭   **ELEVATOR.**

Remember that the pattern for the elevator is given on the A String.
Fingering for this elevator pattern is ___0___ and ___1___ in ___I___ Position.

Going Up

IV String	G	A♭
III String	D	E♭
II String	A	B♭
I String	E	F

Coming Down

I String	F	E
II String	B♭	A
III String	E♭	D
IV String	A♭	G

WRITE THE NOTES FOR THIS ELEVATOR ON THE STAFF.

Remember that what goes *Up* must come *Down*.

Up:

Down:

STUDY GUIDE for Set II Elevator Test—VIOLIN—Set II, no. 2

WRITE THE NOTES FOR THE   B♭   C   **ELEVATOR.**

Remember that the pattern for the elevator is given on the A String.
Fingering for this elevator pattern is ___1___ and ___2___ in ___I___ Position.

Going Up

IV String	A♭	B♭
III String	E♭	F
II String	B♭	C
I String	F	G

Coming Down

I String	G	F
II String	C	B♭
III String	F	E♭
IV String	B♭	A♭

WRITE THE NOTES FOR THIS ELEVATOR ON THE STAFF.

Remember that what goes *Up* must come *Down*.

Up:

Down:

Copyright ©2004 William Dick & Laurie Scott   *Mastery for Strings*

STUDY GUIDE for Set II Elevator Test—VIOLIN—Set II, no. 3

WRITE THE NOTES FOR THE ___C♯___ ___D♯___ **ELEVATOR.**

Remember that the pattern for the elevator is given on the A String.
Fingering for this elevator pattern is ___2___ and ___3___ in ___I___ Position.

Going Up			**Coming Down**		
IV String	B	C♯	I String	A♯	G♯
III String	F♯	G♯	II String	D♯	C♯
II String	C♯	D♯	III String	G♯	F♯
I String	G♯	A♯	IV String	C♯	B

WRITE THE NOTES FOR THIS ELEVATOR ON THE STAFF.

Remember that what goes *Up* must come *Down*.

Up:

Down:

STUDY GUIDE for Set II Elevator Test—VIOLIN—Set II, no. 4

WRITE THE NOTES FOR THE ___D___ ___E___ **ELEVATOR.**

Remember that the pattern for the elevator is given on the A String.
Fingering for this elevator pattern is ___3___ and ___4___ in ___I___ Position.

Going Up			**Coming Down**		
IV String	C	D	I String	B	A
III String	G	A	II String	E	D
II String	D	E	III String	A	G
I String	A	B	IV String	D	C

WRITE THE NOTES FOR THIS ELEVATOR ON THE STAFF.

Remember that what goes *Up* must come *Down*.

Up:

Down:

STUDY GUIDE for Set II Elevator Test—VIOLIN—Set II, no. 5

WRITE THE NOTES FOR THE ___D♯___ ___E___ **ELEVATOR.**

Remember that the pattern for the elevator is given on the A String.
Fingering for this elevator pattern is ___3___ and ___4___ in ___I___ Position.

Going Up

IV String	C♯	D
III String	G♯	A
II String	D♯	E
I String	A♯	B

Coming Down

I String	B	A♯
II String	E	D♯
III String	A	G♯
IV String	D	C♯

WRITE THE NOTES FOR THIS ELEVATOR ON THE STAFF.

Remember that what goes *Up* must come *Down*.

Up:

Down:

STUDY GUIDE for Set II Elevator Test—VIOLIN—Set II, no. 6

WRITE THE NOTES FOR THE ___D___ ___E♭___ **ELEVATOR.**

Remember that the pattern for the elevator is given on the A String.
Fingering for this elevator pattern is ___3___ and ___4___ in ___I___ Position.

Going Up

IV String	C	D♭
III String	G	A♭
II String	D	E♭
I String	A	B♭

Coming Down

I String	B♭	A
II String	E♭	D
III String	E♭	G
IV String	D♭	C

WRITE THE NOTES FOR THIS ELEVATOR ON THE STAFF.

Remember that what goes *Up* must come *Down*.

Up:

Down:

      Mastery for Strings

STUDY GUIDE for Set II Elevator Test—VIOLA—Set II, no. 1

WRITE THE NOTES FOR THE ____A____ ____B♭____ **ELEVATOR.**

Remember that the pattern for the elevator is given on the A String.
Fingering for this elevator pattern is ___0___ and ___1___ in ___I___ Position.

Going Up			**Coming Down**		
IV String	C	D♭	I String	B♭	A
III String	G	A♭	II String	E♭	D
II String	D	E♭	III String	E♭	G
I String	A	B♭	IV String	D♭	C

WRITE THE NOTES FOR THIS ELEVATOR ON THE STAFF.

Remember that what goes *Up* must come *Down*.

Up:

Down:

STUDY GUIDE for Set II Elevator Test—VIOLA—Set II, no. 2

WRITE THE NOTES FOR THE ____B♭____ ____C____ **ELEVATOR.**

Remember that the pattern for the elevator is given on the A String.
Fingering for this elevator pattern is ___1___ and ___2___ in ___I___ Position.

Going Up			**Coming Down**		
IV String	D♭	E♭	I String	C	B♭
III String	A♭	B♭	II String	F	E♭
II String	E♭	F	III String	B♭	A♭
I String	B♭	C	IV String	E♭	D♭

WRITE THE NOTES FOR THIS ELEVATOR ON THE STAFF.

Remember that what goes *Up* must come *Down*.

Up:

Down:

STUDY GUIDE for Set II Elevator Test—VIOLA—Set II, no. 3

WRITE THE NOTES FOR THE _____C♯_____ _____D♯_____ **ELEVATOR.**

Remember that the pattern for the elevator is given on the A String.
Fingering for this elevator pattern is _____2_____ and _____3_____ in _____I_____ Position.

Going Up			**Coming Down**		
IV String	E	F♯	I String	D♯	C♯
III String	B	C♯	II String	G♯	F♯
II String	F♯	G♯	III String	C♯	B
I String	C♯	D♯	IV String	F♯	E

WRITE THE NOTES FOR THIS ELEVATOR ON THE STAFF.

Remember that what goes *Up* must come *Down.*

Up:

Down:

STUDY GUIDE for Set II Elevator Test—VIOLA—Set II, no. 4

WRITE THE NOTES FOR THE _____D_____ _____E_____ **ELEVATOR.**

Remember that the pattern for the elevator is given on the A String.
Fingering for this elevator pattern is _____3_____ and _____4_____ in _____I_____ Position.

Going Up			**Coming Down**		
IV String	F	G	I String	E	D
III String	C	D	II String	A	G
II String	G	A	III String	D	C
I String	D	E	IV String	G	F

WRITE THE NOTES FOR THIS ELEVATOR ON THE STAFF.

Remember that what goes *Up* must come *Down.*

Up:

Down:

     Mastery for Strings

STUDY GUIDE for Set II Elevator Test—VIOLA—Set II, no. 5

WRITE THE NOTES FOR THE ___D♯___ ___E___ **ELEVATOR.**

Remember that the pattern for the elevator is given on the A String.
Fingering for this elevator pattern is ___3___ and ___4___ in ___I___ Position.

Going Up

IV String	F♯	G
III String	C♯	D
II String	G♯	A
I String	D♯	E

Coming Down

I String	E	D♯
II String	A	G♯
III String	D	C♯
IV String	G	F♯

WRITE THE NOTES FOR THIS ELEVATOR ON THE STAFF.

Remember that what goes *Up* must come *Down*.

Up:

Down:

STUDY GUIDE for Set II Elevator Test—VIOLA—Set II, no. 6

WRITE THE NOTES FOR THE ___D___ ___E♭___ **ELEVATOR.**

Remember that the pattern for the elevator is given on the A String.
Fingering for this elevator pattern is ___3___ and ___4___ in ___I___ Position.

Going Up

IV String	F	G♭
III String	C	D♭
II String	G	A♭
I String	D	E♭

Coming Down

I String	E♭	D
II String	A♭	G
III String	D♭	C
IV String	G♭	F

WRITE THE NOTES FOR THIS ELEVATOR ON THE STAFF.

Remember that what goes *Up* must come *Down*.

Up:

Down:

STUDY GUIDE for Set II Elevator Test—CELLO—Set II, no. 1

WRITE THE NOTES FOR THE   __A__   __B♭__   **ELEVATOR.**

Remember that the pattern for the elevator is given on the A String.
Fingering for this elevator pattern is __0__ and __x1__ in __I__ Position.

Going Up			**Coming Down**		
IV String	C	D♭	I String	B♭	A
III String	G	A♭	II String	E♭	D
II String	D	E♭	III String	E♭	G
I String	A	B♭	IV String	D♭	C

WRITE THE NOTES FOR THIS ELEVATOR ON THE STAFF.

Remember that what goes *Up* must come *Down*.

Up:

Down:

STUDY GUIDE for Set II Elevator Test—CELLO—Set II, no. 2

WRITE THE NOTES FOR THE   __B♭__   __C__   **ELEVATOR.**

Remember that the pattern for the elevator is given on the A String.
Fingering for this elevator pattern is __x1__ and __2__ in __I__ Position.

Going Up			**Coming Down**		
IV String	D♭	E♭	I String	C	B♭
III String	A♭	B♭	II String	F	E♭
II String	E♭	F	III String	B♭	A♭
I String	B♭	C	IV String	E♭	D♭

WRITE THE NOTES FOR THIS ELEVATOR ON THE STAFF.

Remember that what goes *Up* must come *Down*.

Up:

Down:

Mastery for Strings

STUDY GUIDE for Set II Elevator Test—CELLO—Set II, no. 3

WRITE THE NOTES FOR THE ___C♯___ ___D♯___ **ELEVATOR.**

Remember that the pattern for the elevator is given on the A String.
Fingering for this elevator pattern is ___x2___ and ___4___ in ___I___ Position.

Going Up

IV String	E	F♯
III String	B	C♯
II String	F♯	G♯
I String	C♯	D♯

Coming Down

I String	D♯	C♯
II String	G♯	F♯
III String	C♯	B
IV String	F♯	E

WRITE THE NOTES FOR THIS ELEVATOR ON THE STAFF.

Remember that what goes *Up* must come *Down*.

Up:

Down:

STUDY GUIDE for Set II Elevator Test—CELLO—Set II, no. 4

WRITE THE NOTES FOR THE ___D___ ___E___ **ELEVATOR.**

Remember that the pattern for the elevator is given on the A String.
Fingering for this elevator pattern is ___2___ and ___4___ in ___II___ Position.

Going Up

IV String	F	G
III String	C	D
II String	G	A
I String	D	E

Coming Down

I String	E	D
II String	A	G
III String	D	C
IV String	G	F

WRITE THE NOTES FOR THIS ELEVATOR ON THE STAFF.

Remember that what goes *Up* must come *Down*.

Up:

Down:

STUDY GUIDE for Set II Elevator Test—CELLO—Set II, no. 5

WRITE THE NOTES FOR THE _D♯_ _E_ **ELEVATOR.**

Remember that the pattern for the elevator is given on the A String.
Fingering for this elevator pattern is __3__ and __4__ in __II__ Position.

Going Up

IV String	F♯	G
III String	C♯	D
II String	G♯	A
I String	D♯	E

Coming Down

I String	E	D♯
II String	A	G♯
III String	D	C♯
IV String	G	F♯

WRITE THE NOTES FOR THIS ELEVATOR ON THE STAFF.

Remember that what goes *Up* must come *Down*.

Up:

Down:

STUDY GUIDE for Set II Elevator Test—CELLO—Set II, no. 6

WRITE THE NOTES FOR THE _D_ _E♭_ **ELEVATOR.**

Remember that the pattern for the elevator is given on the A String.
Fingering for this elevator pattern is __2__ and __3__ in __II__ Position.

Going Up

IV String	F	G♭
III String	C	D♭
II String	G	A♭
I String	D	E♭

Coming Down

I String	E♭	D
II String	A♭	G
III String	D♭	C
IV String	G♭	F

WRITE THE NOTES FOR THIS ELEVATOR ON THE STAFF.

Remember that what goes *Up* must come *Down*.

Up:
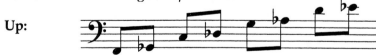

Down:

 Mastery for Strings

STUDY GUIDE for Set II Elevator Test—STRING BASS—Set II, no. 1

WRITE THE NOTES FOR THE <u>A</u> <u>B♭</u> **ELEVATOR.**

Remember that the pattern for the elevator is given on the A String.
Fingering for this elevator pattern is <u>0</u> and <u>1</u> in <u>1/2</u> Position.

Going Up			**Coming Down**		
IV String	E	F	I String	A♭	G
III String	A	B♭	II String	E♭	D
II String	D	E♭	III String	B♭	A
I String	G	A♭	IV String	F	E

WRITE THE NOTES FOR THIS ELEVATOR ON THE STAFF.

Remember that what goes *Up* must come *Down*.

Up:

Down:

STUDY GUIDE for Set II Elevator Test—STRING BASS—Set II, no. 2

WRITE THE NOTES FOR THE <u>B♭</u> <u>C</u> **ELEVATOR.**

Remember that the pattern for the elevator is given on the A String.
Fingering for this elevator pattern is <u>1</u> and <u>4</u> in <u>1/2</u> Position.

Going Up			**Coming Down**		
IV String	F	G	I String	B♭	A♭
III String	B♭	C	II String	F	E♭
II String	E♭	F	III String	C	B♭
I String	A♭	B♭	IV String	G	F

WRITE THE NOTES FOR THIS ELEVATOR ON THE STAFF.

Remember that what goes *Up* must come *Down*.

Up:

Down:

STUDY GUIDE for Set II Elevator Test—STRING BASS—Set II, no. 3

WRITE THE NOTES FOR THE _____C♯_____ _____D♯_____ **ELEVATOR.**

Remember that the pattern for the elevator is given on the A String.
Fingering for this elevator pattern is _____1_____ and _____4_____ in _____II_____ Position.

Going Up			**Coming Down**		
IV String	G♯	A♯	I String	C♯	B
III String	C♯	D♯	II String	G♯	F♯
II String	F♯	G♯	III String	D♯	C♯
I String	B	C♯	IV String	A♯	G♯

WRITE THE NOTES FOR THIS ELEVATOR ON THE STAFF.

Remember that what goes *Up* must come *Down*.

Up:

Down:

STUDY GUIDE for Set II Elevator Test—STRING BASS—Set II, no. 4

WRITE THE NOTES FOR THE _____D_____ _____E_____ **ELEVATOR.**

Remember that the pattern for the elevator is given on the A String.
Fingering for this elevator pattern is _____1_____ and _____4_____ in _____III_____ Position.

Going Up			**Coming Down**		
IV String	A	B	I String	D	C
III String	D	E	II String	A	G
II String	G	A	III String	E	D
I String	C	D	IV String	B	A

WRITE THE NOTES FOR THIS ELEVATOR ON THE STAFF.

Remember that what goes *Up* must come *Down*.

Up:

Down:

  Mastery for Strings

STUDY GUIDE for Set II Elevator Test—STRING BASS—Set II, no. 5
WRITE THE NOTES FOR THE _____D♯_____ _____E_____ **ELEVATOR.**

Remember that the pattern for the elevator is given on the A String.
Fingering for this elevator pattern is ___2___ and ___4___ in ___III___ Position.

Going Up			**Coming Down**		
IV String	A♯	B	I String	D	C♯
III String	D♯	E	II String	A	G♯
II String	G♯	A	III String	E	D♯
I String	C♯	D	IV String	B	A♯

WRITE THE NOTES FOR THIS ELEVATOR ON THE STAFF.

Remember that what goes *Up* must come *Down*.

Up:

Down:

STUDY GUIDE for Set II Elevator Test—STRING BASS—Set II, no. 6
WRITE THE NOTES FOR THE _____D_____ _____E♭_____ **ELEVATOR.**

Remember that the pattern for the elevator is given on the A String.
Fingering for this elevator pattern is ___1___ and ___2___ in ___III___ Position.

Going Up			**Coming Down**		
IV String	A	B♭	I String	D♭	C
III String	D	E♭	II String	A♭	G
II String	G	A♭	III String	E♭	D
I String	C	D♭	IV String	B♭	A

WRITE THE NOTES FOR THIS ELEVATOR ON THE STAFF.

Remember that what goes Up must come Down.

Up:

Down:

EXPRESS ELEVATORS: SET II
Mastery #35, continued

THINGS YOU WILL LEARN

✔ The names of the notes in each elevator pattern.

✔ How to play the elevator pattern in tune across the fingerboard.

✔ How to play across the fingerboard and have one fingercut.

✔ How to slur across the entire fingerboard with smooth arm motion.

RULES FOR PLAYING

Separate bows:
1. Say the name of all the notes in the elevator, up and down, before you play.
2. After playing the elevator check to see that you have only one fingercut on each finger.
3. Remember to use walking fingers as you cross the fingerboard.

Slurred bows:
1. Say the name of all the notes in the elevator, up and down, before you play.
2. After playing the elevator check to see that you have only one fingercut on each finger.
3. Remember to use walking fingers as you cross the fingerboard.
4. The frog of your bow should make a smooth arc as you slur across the strings.
5. The bow should not "click" from one string level to the next string level.

To Achieve Mastery: ride each of the elevator patterns on all four strings, saying the name of the notes before you play them and have only one fingercut on each finger.

Set II Elevators: Remember that the pattern is given on the A string.
1. A - B♭
2. B♭ - C
3. C♯ - D♯
4. D - E
5. D♯ - E
6. D - E♭

Mastery for Strings

Remember that the notenames for the patterns are given on the A string.

Separate bows

Slurred Express Elevators

EXPRESS ELEVATOR SET II—VIOLA—MASTERY #35

Remember that the notenames for the patterns are given on the A string.

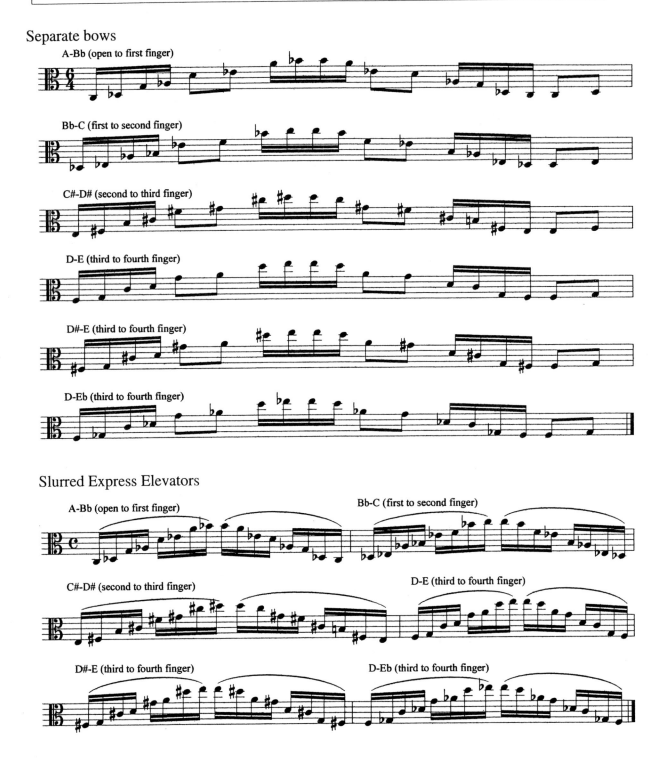

Separate bows

A-Bb (open to first finger)

Bb-C (first to second finger)

C#-D# (second to third finger)

D-E (third to fourth finger)

D#-E (third to fourth finger)

D-Eb (third to fourth finger)

Slurred Express Elevators

A-Bb (open to first finger)

Bb-C (first to second finger)

C#-D# (second to third finger)

D-E (third to fourth finger)

D#-E (third to fourth finger)

D-Eb (third to fourth finger)

 Mastery for Strings

Remember that the notenames for the patterns are given on the A string.

Separate bows

Slurred Express Elevators

EXPRESS ELEVATOR SET II
STRING BASS, SOLO VERSION—MASTERY #35

Remember that the notenames for the patterns are given on the A string.

Separate bows

Slurred Express Elevators

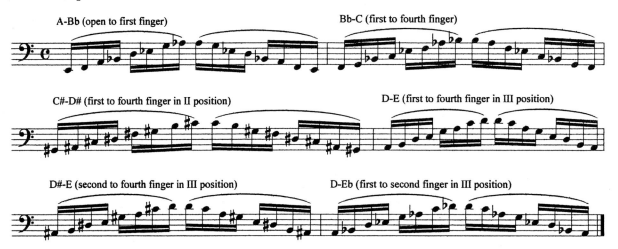

Copyright ©2004 William Dick & Laurie Scott   *Mastery for Strings*

EXPRESS ELEVATOR SET II
STRING BASS, CLASS VERSION—MASTERY #35

Remember that the notenames for the patterns are given on the A string.

Separate bows

Slurred Express Elevators

TICK-TOCK TWINKLE
Mastery #36

THINGS YOU WILL LEARN

- ✔ How to play with a metronome.
- ✔ How to play sixteenth notes ♫♫ ♫♫ .
- ✔ How to play eighth notes ♫ ♫ .
- ✔ How to play quarter notes ♩ ♩ .
- ✔ How to make smooth sounds (legato) and stopped sounds (staccato) with your bow.
- ✔ How to articulate the bow in "Baroque" style.

RULES FOR PLAYING

1. Turn the metronome on to: quarter note equals 60. The metronome will click once each second.

2. Play ♫♫ ♫♫ (rubaduba, rubaduba) on the first note of Twinkle (D). The bow should make a smooth (legato) sound. You will play four bows for each click of the metronome.

3. Play ♫ ♫ (tick-tick-tick-tick) on the second note of Twinkle (A). Each bow stroke should have a strong "T" sound at the beginning of the stroke, and a strong "K" sound at the end of the stroke to make a stopped (staccato) sound. You will play two bows for each click of the metronome.

4. Play ♫♫ ♫♫ (rubaduba, rubaduba) on the third note of Twinkle (B). The bow should make a smooth (legato) sound. You will play four bows for each click of the metronome.

5. Play ♩ ♩ (TOCK - TOCK) on the fourth note of Twinkle (A). Each bow stroke should have a strong "T" sound at the beginning of the stroke, and a strong "K" sound at the end of the stroke to make a stopped (staccato) sound. You will play one bow for each click of the metronome.

6. Continue the rotation of rubaduba, rubaduba; tick-tick-tick-tick; rubaduba, rubaduba; TOCK - TOCK; through all the notes of Twinkle.

To Achieve Mastery: play Tick-Tock Twinkle with a smooth (legato) bow stroke for all the ♫♫ ♫♫ sixteenth notes, and a stopped (staccato) bow stroke for all the ♫♫ eighth and ♩ ♩ quarter notes. The staccato strokes must have a strong "T" sound at the beginning of each stroke and a strong "K" sound at the end of each stroke.

 Mastery for Strings

METRONOME TWINKLE BREAD
Mastery #37

THINGS YOU WILL LEARN

✔ How to subdivide a beat into rhythmic parts.

✔ How to play the subdivisions of a beat with the metronome.

✔ How to internalize the mathematical ratios of subdivisions of a beat.

✔ That a beat can be subdivide into two parts called eighth notes.

✔ That a beat can be subdivide into three parts called triplets.

✔ That a beat can be subdivide into four parts called sixteenth notes.

✔ A method of counting subdivisions of a beat called "rhythmic counting."

RULES FOR PLAYING

1. Play the "Bread" recipe of Twinkle (the first phrase) with four bows on each note of the recipe. (D-D-D-D-/A-A-A-A-/B-B-B-B-/A-A-A-A-/etc.).

2. Set the metronome at quarter note = 60. That means that the metronome will click one time each second.

3. Repeat the first phrase of Twinkle (step one) and make sure that your bow changes exactly with the metronome. You will be playing quarter notes at MM=60.

4. Repeat step three but now subdivide each quarter note into two eighth notes. You will now play eight notes in the same time as it took to play four quarter notes.

5. Repeat step three but now subdivide each quarter note into three triplets. You will now play twelve notes in the same time as it took to play four quarter notes.

6. Repeat step three but now subdivide each quarter note into four sixteenth notes. You will now play sixteen notes in the same time as it took to play four quarter notes.

Rhythmic Counting:

When you play the first phrase of Twinkle in quarter notes you count
1   2   3   4

When you play the first phrase of Twinkle in eighth notes you count
1   and   2   and   3   and   4   and

When you play the first phrase of Twinkle in triplets you count
1   la   lee   2   la   lee   3   la   lee   4   la   lee

When you play the first phrase of Twinkle in sixteenth notes you count
1 tah tay tah   2 tah tay tah   3 tah tay tah   4 tah tay tah

To Achieve Mastery: play the first phrase of Twinkle in quarters, eighths, triplets, and sixteenths with the metronome set at MM=60. Say the rhythmic counting syllables as you play.

CHROMATIC ESCALATOR
Masteries #38, 39 & 40

THINGS YOU WILL LEARN

✔ How to play all the notes on your instrument that are in First Position.

✔ How to hear and play a scale that has all the notes a half-step apart.

✔ How to develop flexible joints in your fingers.

✔ How to name the notes of your instrument using both "sharp" and "flat" names.

✔ What "enharmonic spelling" means.

RULES FOR PLAYING THE CHROMATIC ESCALATOR SONG

1. Start on the lowest string on your instrument and go all the way to the top of the escalator pattern. Repeat the top note and come down the escalator.

2. Say the name of the note before you play it.

3 Say and play the Chromatic Escalator Song using only the "sharp" name of notes.

4 Say and play the Chromatic Escalator Song using only the "flat" name of notes.

5. Say and play the Chromatic Escalator Song using the "sharp" names on the way up and the "flat" names on the way down.

Chromatic Escalator Patterns

Mastery # 38—

A String	A	A♯	B	C	C♯	D	D♯	E	
violin/viola fingerings	0	1	1	2	2	3	3	4	
cello fingering	0	1	1	2	2	3	4	1	(Shift to IV Pos.)
string bass fingering	0	1	1	2	4	0	1	1	
	A	B♭	B	C	D♭	D	E♭	E	

D String	D	D♯	E	F	F♯	G	G♯	A	
violin/viola fingerings	0	1	1	2	2	3	3	4	
cello fingering	0	1	1	2	2	3	4	1	(Shift to IV Pos.)
string bass fingering	0	1	1	2	4	0	1	1	
	D	E♭	E	F	G♭	G	A♭	A	

Mastery # 39—

G String	G	G♯	A	A♯	B	C	C♯	D	
violin/viola fingerings	0	1	1	2	2	3	3	4	
cello fingering	0	1	1	2	2	3	4	1	(Shift to IV Pos.)
string bass fingering	0	1	1	2	4	1	2	4	(Shift to III Pos.)
	G	A♭	A	B♭	B	C	D♭	D	

C String	C	C♯	D	D♯	E	F	F♯	G	
viola fingerings	0	1	1	2	2	3	3	4	
cello fingering	0	1	1	2	2	3	4	1	(Shift to IV Pos.)
	C	D♭	D	E♭	E	F	G♭	G	

E String	E	F	F♯	G	G♯	A	A♯	B	
violin/viola fingerings	0	1	1	2	2	3	3	4	
string bass fingering	0	1	1	2	4	0	1	1	
	E	F	G♭	G	A♭	A	B♭	B	

To Achieve Mastery: ride the escalator up and down the assigned strings and have only one fingercut on each finger.

Mastery # 40— To Achieve Mastery on the Express Chromatic Escalator: start on your lowest open string and ride the chromatic escalator across all four strings for two octaves.

Copyright ©2001 William Dick & Laurie Scott   *Mastery for Strings*

ONE-OCTAVE SCALES, SET III
Mastery #41

THINGS YOU WILL LEARN

✔ What a scale is.

✔ What the word "octave" means.

✔ How to play a "Major Scale."

RULES FOR PLAYING

1. Say the name of the pitch before you play it.
2. Play the ♪♪♪ ♩♩ rhythm on each note of the scale.
3. When you reach the top pitch, repeat that pitch and then play back down the scale.

DEFINITIONS

- A scale is a series of consecutive pitches.
- An octave is the pitch eight notes higher or lower from the starting pitch. Since we only use seven letters of the alphabet, the name of the octave pitch is always the same as the beginning pitch.

SCALE SET III

Violins:
- C   (start 3rd finger on G)
- F   (start 2nd finger on D)
- F♯   (start 2nd finger on D)
- B♭   (start 2nd finger on G)

Violas:
- F   (start 3rd finger on C)
- B♭   (start 2nd finger on G)
- B   (start 2nd finger on G)
- E♭   (start 2nd finger on C)

Cellos:
- F   (start 4th finger on C)
- B♭   (start 2nd finger on G)
- E♭   (start 2nd finger on C, with 2nd finger extension on G string)
- B   (start with extended 2nd finger on G)

String Basses:
- F   (start 1st finger in half position on E)
- F♯   (start 1st finger in first position on E)
- B♭   (start 1st finger in half position on A)
- B   (start 1st finger in first position on A)

To Achieve Mastery: you may look at the "Key Signatures and Scales" on the next page to perform the scales for your instrument with no mistakes.

KEY SIGNATURES AND SCALES

C MAJOR

| C | D | E | F | G | A | B | C |

G MAJOR (one sharp)

| G | A | B | C | D | E | F♯ | G |

D MAJOR (two sharps)

| D | E | F♯ | G | A | B | C♯ | D |

A MAJOR (three sharps)

| A | B | C♯ | D | E | F♯ | G♯ | A |

E MAJOR (four sharps)

| E | F♯ | G♯ | A | B | C♯ | D♯ | E |

B MAJOR (five sharps)

| B | C♯ | D♯ | E | F♯ | G♯ | A♯ | B |

F MAJOR (one flat)

| F | G | A | B♭ | C | D | E | F |

B-FLAT MAJOR (two flats)

| B♭ | C | D | E♭ | F | G | A | B♭ |

E-FLAT MAJOR (three flats)

| E♭ | F | G | A♭ | B♭ | C | D | E♭ |

A-FLAT MAJOR (four flats)

| A♭ | B♭ | C | D♭ | E♭ | F | G | A♭ |

D-FLAT MAJOR (five flats)

| D♭ | E♭ | F | G♭ | A♭ | B♭ | C | D♭ |

F-SHARP MAJOR (six sharps)

| F♯ | G♯ | A♯ | B | C♯ | D♯ | E♯ | F♯ |

C-SHARP MAJOR (seven sharps)

| C♯ | D♯ | E♯ | F♯ | G♯ | A♯ | B♯ | C♯ |

Copyright ©2004 William Dick & Laurie Scott *Mastery for Strings*

One-Octave Scales, Set III

Arabic numbers (1) indicate finger.
Roman numbers (I) indicate position.

Cello

String Bass

ONE-OCTAVE SCALES, SET IV
Mastery #42

THINGS YOU WILL LEARN

- ✔ What a scale is.
- ✔ What the word "octave" means.
- ✔ How to play a "Major Scale."

RULES FOR PLAYING

1. Say the name of the pitch before you play it.
2. Play the ♫♫ ♩♩ rhythm on each note of the scale.
3. When you reach the top pitch, repeat that pitch and then play back down the scale.

DEFINITIONS

- A scale is a series of consecutive pitches.
- An octave is the pitch eight notes higher or lower from the starting pitch. Since we only use seven letters of the alphabet, the name of the octave pitch is always the same as the beginning pitch.

SCALE SET IV

Violins:	A♭	(start 1st finger on G)
	E♭	(start 1st finger on D)
	D♭	(start 4th finger on G)
Violas:	D♭	(start 1st finger on C)
	A♭	(start 1st finger on G)
	F♯	(start 3rd finger on C)
Cellos:	C♯	(start 4th finger on G)
	F♯	(start 4th finger on C)
	A♭	(start 1st finger on G, with shifts to 2nd position on both G and D)
String Basses:	A♭	(start 4th finger on E)
	D♭	(start 4th finger on A)
	E♭	(start 1st finger in half position on D)

To Achieve Mastery: you may look at the "Key Signatures and Scales" page to perform the scales for your instrument with no mistakes.

Mastery for Strings

ONE-OCTAVE SCALES, SET IV

Arabic numbers (1) indicate finger.
Roman numbers (I) indicate position.

Cello

String Bass

CERTIFICATE OF MASTERY

This is to certify that

_____

has completed the sequence
of technical skills necessary to achieve

Level One Mastery

for

_____.

Congratulations!

Teacher: _____   Date: _____